MR. COPPING – A MASTER TEACHER

Mr. Copping – A Master Teacher

Born 7 May 1903
Pupil-Teacher 1917-1921
College Student 1922-1924
Assistant Teacher 1924-1937
College Tutor 1937-1968
Died 28 September 1985

David Lodge

William Sessions Limited
York, England

ISBN 1 85072 181 5

Printed in 11 on 11½ point Plantin Typeface
from Author's Disk
by Sessions of York
The Ebor Press
York, England

Contents

Illustrations

Foreword

IT IS A PLEASURE and privilege to commend this account of the life of Joseph Copping – dear friend and colleague for many years. David Lodge has put us all in his debt for this labour of love in recalling the many aspects of Joe's life.

When I came to St. John's after the war, it was Joe who introduced me to the College with its handful of faithful tutors and its somewhat rigidly disciplined life. I had never in all my life met anyone like Joe. He had immense energy and unique powers of concentration with real imaginative flair. He helped to make the social life of the College enjoyable and to break down the barriers between tutors and students. His Saturday Evening Music Circles were hugely enjoyed and until the Disco era his Saturday Night Dances were a great success.

In Education – a word I rarely heard him use – he was unique and his work with Primary School classes drew widespread admiration. Open-plan classrooms and individual child-centred studies meant little to him. He knew that a teacher was not to be a neutral provider of materials – but a vital, energetic and imaginative worker who loved children and made their education efficient and enjoyable.

Enjoyment was a Keyword to Joe whether in the classroom, the dance hall or a foreign holiday – as well as the word Jolly. He brought happiness and enjoyment wherever he went and the College and those whom helped owe him an immense debt of gratitude.

Christopher Chapman

Introduction

AN AUTOBIOGRAPHY IS something different. Often, the writer of such a work wants the world to know what a very special kind of person they are or were, what wonderful things he or she has done for the human race or has a strong desire to be immortalised.

Joseph Copping was not that sort of person. More than once he refused point blank to write down the events of his life when pressed to do so by the writer of the story which follows – 'Who wants to know about me when I'm dead' was his typically down-to-earth reply. Only once in his life-time did he publicly speak briefly of his childhood and upbringing when he talked to a group of college students about 'A Chapel in Norfolk', and then only after being strongly persuaded to do so by one of his close colleagues. Joe was a man of 'today', never one of 'yesterday', and certainly not one who considered what he was doing as anything other than a straightforward 'job of work'.

His 'job-of-work' was that of a teacher, a lifetime spent educating others, and by the word 'educate' I mean it in the fullest sense – nourishing and rearing the *whole* person, not merely cramming facts into people's brains. Joe got to *know* pupils and students as individuals better than many members of staff, which accounts for the fact that so many of them remember him more readily than any other teachers and tutors who taught them during their time at school or college. That, indeed, is the measure of someone very special.

Those who came into contact with Mr. Copping will not forget him, and for them no book needs to be written, but for those who did not know Joe I believe that to read his life's work could prove to be an inspiration that should live on, an example that may help future generations of teachers to realise that there is more to 'education' that just standing in front of a class and talking.

The compilation of this Biography has not been easy, in more ways than one, but I have been very fortunate in the help and information I have received from Joe's former colleagues, from the many references recorded in the College magazines, and from some of his personal papers which he entrusted into my keeping. Without this help, which is acknowledged elsewhere, the undertaking would have been impossible.

J.R.C. was a truly complex man whose many faceted talents, skills, and abilities, to say nothing of his vitality, humanity and sheer capacity for work, merged daily into what can only be described as a human dynamo. He was constantly engaged in so many areas of school and college life that, of necessity, they have had to be separated under different headings in order to do them justice. In 'life' these arbitrary divisions did not exist – each and every activity was interwoven into Joe's daily routine and he took them all in his stride with an ease which was amazing to witness. I hope the fragmentation will not distract the reader's attention from the overall view of Joe's true personality nor detract from the picture I have tried to paint of him. I am, after a period of ten years since he passed away, still not sure whether he would have wanted me to pen this work but the deed is now done and, I trust, is 'done well'.

Having said that, I am very conscious of the fact that what has been written, or edited from that already said or written about Joseph Robert Copping's life, does little more than embrace a mere fraction of what he put into life, what he *gave* of himself to others, what inspiration he radiated or what knowledge he imparted.

The sheer magnitude of trying to tell the story of this truly 'great' man was a challenge, a challenge which it has been a privilege to meet. What has emerged is a collation of some of his own works with many other people's thoughts and words, woven together by my own inadequate additions. It was an honour to have known Joe, both as a revered tutor and as a very good friend, and I hope this work, in some small way, repays the gratitude, admiration and respect I owe to him.

Joseph R. Copping – long may **your** 'Light shine before men, that they may see your good works, and glorify your Father, which is in Heaven'. [St. Matthew, Ch. 5, v.16]

David Lodge
Holgate
February 1996

Acknowledgements

FIRST AND FOREMOST I thank my wife Judy for her patience in putting up with the 'mess' created by my having papers, photographs and magazines scattered all over my home 'office' for such a long time and for supplying me with innumerable cups of tea to keep me going.

To Christopher Chapman I say a very big thank you for giving your time to read the draft scripts, for your encouragement, helpful suggestions, and additional material and for writing the Foreword.

Stanley Barnes kindly provided me with information about the Variety shows and with photographs, amongst other things, Leonard Poore gave me the tape recording of 'A Chapel in Norfolk' and Patrick Hunter very kindly drew the plans of the Manor School and St. John's, using CAD – my grateful thanks to you all.

Audrey James has been a pillar of strength in copying out entries concerning Joe from the Manor School Log Book and from *The White Rose* and *Spread Eagle*. She has also proof-read the final script and helped in other ways. My thanks to you Audrey.

My grateful thanks to John Maw for helping me with research into the College magazines, to Mr. Peter Smith, the Headmaster of the Manor School, for his courtesy in allowing me to examine and copy information from the School Log Book, to David Glew for the information he gave me about his time as a student at The Croft and to James Dyer for his contribution about holidays abroad and for photographs.

I found Principal G. P. McGregor's book, *A Church College for the 21st Century*, provided me with a flavour of College life during the early part of this century, which was a great help.

To the many Old Johnsmen who wrote to me about Joe, or others who have assisted in any way but whom I have not named, I extend my thanks.

Finally, I wish to thank Mr. Richard York of Sessions of York, for his courtesy and the very practical help he has provided in bringing this book to fruition.

For any errors in the words I have written, or omissions (and no doubt there will be many), I take the full blame. I hope they do not detract too much from your reading.

CHAPTER I

Early Days

'JOE COPPING IS THE only genius I know personally' .... so said Stanley Watkin, one-time bursar at St. John's College, York, of a man who was about to retire from almost a lifetime of teaching.

High praise indeed coming from Stanley who was not known to exaggerate nor to mince his words. So, who was this 'genius'? Did he really deserve the accolade? The reader will be left to decide.

Joseph Robert Copping was born on the 7th May 1903 in the village of Worstead in Norfolk, a place whose main claim to fame, apart from being the birthplace of Joe, is that it gave its name to the fine woollen cloth, introduced into England by the Flemish weavers who were brought over from the continent by Edward III and settled there in the thirteenth century.

In the words of Joe, his mother and father were 'getting on a bit' when he arrived on the scene and, as he recalled during a talk given to College students in 1966 entitled 'A Chapel in Norfolk', the name Joseph was given to him because he was 'an addition'. His father, James Benjamin Copping, was a 57-year-old grocer and draper at the time of Joe's birth and his mother was James' second wife and eleven years his junior. Joe had four step-brothers and a step-sister, all twenty years or more older than himself so many of his youthful days, living virtually as an 'only child', were spent helping his parents in their 'emporium' at Norwich House, where the family lived over the shop.

Joe's paternal grandfather was born in 1789, the year of the French Revolution and he became a father for the twenty-third time in 1846 at the age of fifty-seven when his youngest son James Benjamin was born. Grandfather Copping was a miller at Hardwick and Joe's father, James, worked for him for many years carrying sacks of corn and flour and generally busying himself in the everyday working life of the mill. However, he always yearned to be his own master one day and in particular to be a grocer. Eventually in 1883 James, who by this time was a widower, moved from Hardwick to Worstead where he had seen a Post Office cum grocery and drapery store advertised as being for sale. Having bought this enormous, once thatched, rambling fourteenth century weavers' house and garden he found to his great dismay that there was no Methodist Chapel in the village.

James was a very fervent Primitive Methodist so the thought of going to Worstead church was an anathema to him. When he first took up residence in his new house he was obliged to walk several miles every Sunday to worship in the nearest chapel but he was not content with this arrangement and wanted to build a chapel in his own village. First he had to find a way of raising sufficient money to pay for such a building so, obviously being a man of action rather than words (like father, like son!) he organised a group of like-minded believers into a musical band, began by raising money for their uniforms and instruments (he actually made some of the violins himself) and afterwards gave performances all around the area over a period of four years and succeeded in raising £300.

He then looked around for a suitable plot of land to buy, but the village 'squire' Colonel Rous and an indomitable lady by the name of Mrs. Russell Day who was propelled round the village in a Bath chair, both powerful local landowners, made sure that James was unable to purchase any. Furthermore the vicar, the Rev. Breffitt, had made it quite clear to everyone that, as the church was capable of holding 1,400 souls, he saw no reason at all for having any other place of worship in Worstead.

Joe's father was not to be beaten by the local hierarchy so he had the new chapel built on a piece of his own land behind the house, in what was the back garden, and next to the outside loo! He and others of a similar persuasion could now practise their faith in the village in the building which soon became known as Copping's Chapel. Not only had James achieved his ambition but he had saved himself a great deal of travel every Sunday!

Having sorted out the religious side of his life satisfactorily James could now concentrate fully on secular matters by working hard in the now flourishing business at Norwich House. He remarried a lady of eleven years his junior and in 1903 baby Joseph arrived – rather unexpectedly!

Mr. and Mrs. James Copping.

Of his formative years there is no evidence other than the stories Joe used to relate about going with his father or his step-sister Flo to meet the mail-coach at 4.30 a.m. each morning and bringing back the sack of letters to the shop, where they were sorted and delivered to the people in the village. He spoke of helping his mother and father in the store both before and during his school days and later when he was a pupil-teacher. At this time the shop opened at eight o'clock in the morning and closed at eight in the evening, Mondays to Fridays remaining open until 10.00 p.m. on Saturdays. Joe also spoke of his and his family's involvement with the Chapel 'in the back garden' of which more later.

Mr. James Copping, whom Joe said had only two enemies, the Pope and the Devil was as you may imagine a typical Victorian father with high moral standards and a strong desire that his family should walk 'in the ways of the Lord'. He was a strict disciplinarian and an honest tradesman and Joe said he was always fair in his judgements and 'you knew where you were with him'. His photograph taken at about the time Joe was born shows him with balding forehead and neatly trimmed hair, a full moustache and kindly mouth but with keen perceptive deep-set eyes.

There is no mistaking the fact from the photograph that Mrs. Copping was Joe's mother! His features were to grow into an almost identical replica of hers even down to that rather impish look which could at any time break out into a wry smile. Her neat boyish hairstyle indicates a strictly practical woman who had more important things to do than spend time in front of a mirror tending to long hair. Joe described her as a truly indefatigable lady who never took a holiday in her life.

And so Joe grew up and was soon attending the Worstead village Church of England School as one of forty-five pupils. Two of his contemporaries in the senior section were Fred Loads, who later became famous as one of the panel on Gardener's Question Time, and Charles Forder, later to become the Venerable Archdeacon of York. In 1917, when Joe was fourteen-years-old and coming to the end of his compulsory education, his teacher Mrs. Colthorpe asked the members of the senior class if there was anyone who wanted to become a teacher and on informing his mother of this she thought it would be a 'good idea'. It was then, in Joe's words, 'That the rot set in!' Joe said he had always wanted to be a gardener but instead was to begin his training as a pupil-teacher at the same school he had been about to leave.

CHAPTER II

Pupil-Teacher

AFTER THE MOMENTOUS decision had been jointly made by Joe's teacher, Mrs. Colthorpe and his mother that 'it would be a good idea' for him to become a teacher he was obliged, as an elementary school pupil, to become a pupil-teacher in order to matriculate before he could attend a college. As a fourteen-year-old having to face four years extra study plus another two at college must have seemed a daunting prospect. Looking back on it in later years Joe described his four extra years at Worstead school as 'a hard grind' and he would not have said that lightly.

The pupil-teacher came under the direct supervision of the headteacher, in Joe's case Mr. T. H. Ford and the 'apprenticeship' consisted of assisting other teachers with their classes, preparing and teaching two 'Criticism' lessons per week to various classes, under the watchful eye of the headmaster, teaching other lessons and at the same time studying several subjects to a higher level in preparation for matriculation.

The author is very fortunate in having in his possession a small Norfolk Education Committee Exercise Book in which the seventeen-year-old Joe wrote a dozen of his 'Criticism Lessons' during 1920/1921. All are set out with the Aims and Introduction, then the Matter and the Method written side by side on a divided page, with the B.Bd.S. [Blackboard summary] and where appropriate with sketch map(s) or diagrams which were to be used during the lesson, towards the end. All are written in 'copperplate' handwriting and all except one has a criticism written and signed by the headmaster on the final page. [Anyone who was taught by Joe in the Primary Education sessions will be able to look at replicas of this type of lesson preparation in their own 'Front-and Back' books if, like me, they have kept them.]

Joe certainly came in for some hard criticism from Mr. Ford. The first example in the notebook of a 'Copy Writing' lesson given to Standards 1 and 2 on 15th September 1920 is concluded by these words –

Criticism 15/9/20

> Notes Fairly full & f'ly well arranged, but writing is extremely poor & slovenly. Take more care with your writing or it will soon become unreadable.
> Class Order was Good. Chn. were kept well at work. Attention is needed in formation of the letter 'r' in several cases.
> Rather too long taken for such a small quantity of work from chn. Let chn. write at least two copies.
>
> (Signed) T. H. Ford
> 15/9/20

The first of two lessons on 'Day and Night' initially given by Joe to Standards 5, 6 and 7 on the 20th October 1920 comes in for two full pages of the headmaster's notes with the demand that it must be repeated.

Criticism 20/10/20

> These notes are very poorly written & not at all tidy. Much better attempt (will be attempted) [words in brackets crossed out. Ed.] must be made next time.
> Tr's. grammar still needs care e.g. 'That is not what the earth do'.
> * 'Now' still too frequently used to introduce speech.
> Several questions were quite 'backhanded' e.g. 'Why does earth turn round this way?' – This was not understood by one child.
> More use should have been made of candle & ball (or apple) before making any mention whatever of the earth or of day and night.
> Then globe should have been used. Chn. would then have been able to understand & answer questions. As it was most of class were quite 'in the dark' as to what questions meant. – in fact if chn. understood lesson they were smarter than I ever give them credit for.
> This lesson will be repeated with Stds. III & IV, with fresh notes etc. after a specimen lesson by Hd.Tr. to Stds. I & II.
>
> (Signed) T. H. Ford
> 20/10/20

Reading this criticism carefully reveals that there must have been a spark of humour in Mr. Ford's makeup – how many good teachers are there without some at least? Nonetheless he must have been a hard taskmaster. The 'repeat' lesson, written up by Joe on the 27th October 1920 and most likely given the next day is reproduced on the pages following together with the Head's criticism, which unusually within the notebook, is not signed and dated.

It may seem rather cruel and 'below the belt' to resurrect some of the adverse comments made about Joe's work during his training but it is done with no other reason than to illustrate the kind of detailed preparation he was obliged to undertake and the scrutiny to which his early teaching experience was subjected. There is no doubt that it helped Joe to develop into what he was to become – an outstanding teacher and tutor. However, he took on a rather different approach and spent his entire working life gently guiding others to learn by example and encouragement rather than by criticism.

But to return to the notebook and those criticisms, most of which it must be admitted have an element of 'constructive' as well as critical comment. A lesson on 'Canada' given on the 21st September to Standards 1 & 2 elicits the following comments:

> Teacher attempts too much in time allowed. Instead of trying to teach 'everything' about Canada a 'Voyage to and a Journey Across Canada' would have been better. A liner and an American train could both have been described and compared with small ships and trains chn. had seen.
> A modern liner and its speed etc. could also have been compared with a sailing ship. Then other lessons could follow.
> Matter in notes is sufficient for several lessons.
> Method: Don't tell chn. everything you are going to do – 'I am going to write that on the board'. – 'I am going to tell you about that later'.
> Teacher endeavoured to keep all at work and tried to make lesson interesting, – some chn. still require a deal of rousing, – some give little or no attention.
> Next lesson to be taken with another class.

'Scottish Lakes' form the basis of a lesson delivered to Standards 3 & 4 on October 13th. Duration of lesson is 30 mins. and the Aims are – To interest chrn. in the Geog. of the highlands; To train observation and maintain interest throughout the lesson; To test chrn's knowledge of mountains and formation of lakes.

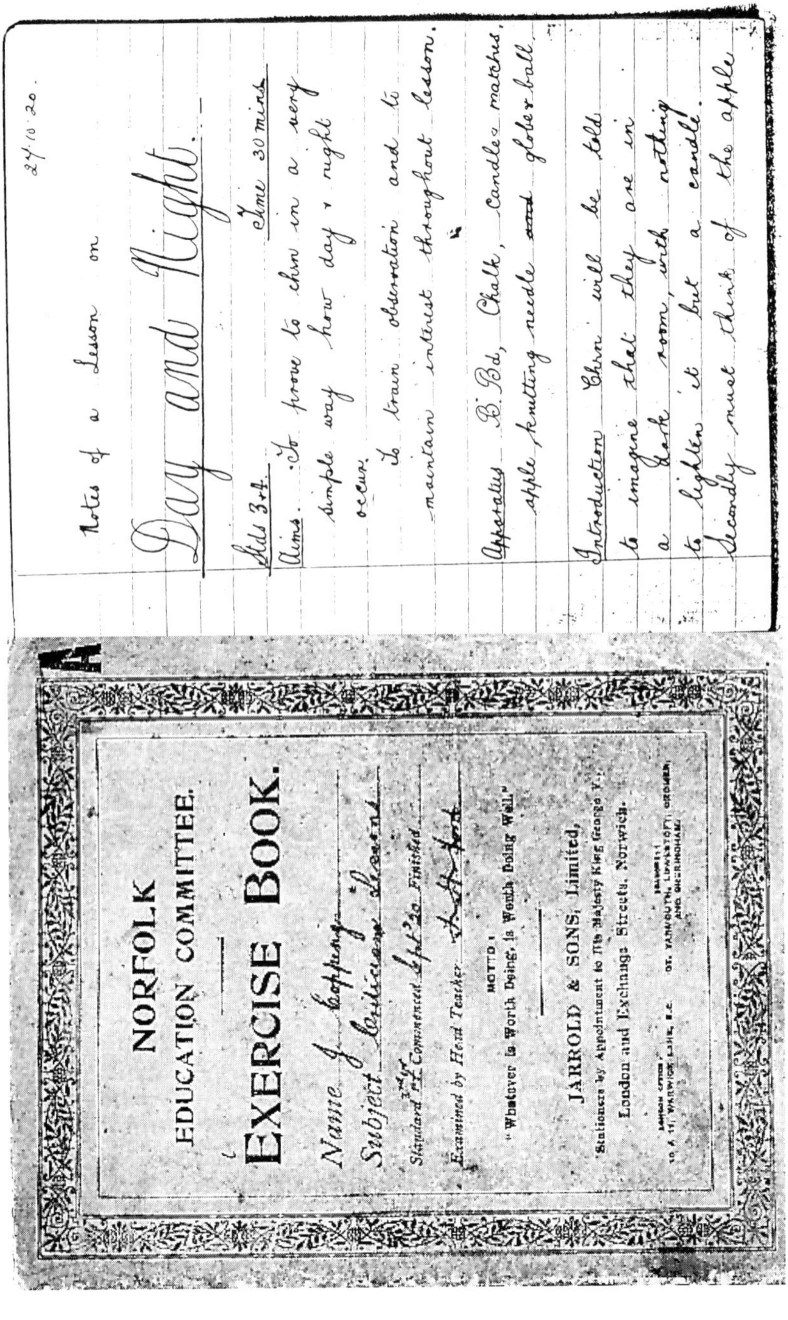
NORFOLK
EDUCATION COMMITTEE.
EXERCISE BOOK.
Name
Subject Criticism Lessons
Standard Commenced Sept 20 Finished
Examined by Head Teacher
MOTTO:
"Whatever is Worth Doing, is Worth Doing Well."
JARROLD & SONS, Limited,
Stationers by Appointment to His Majesty King George V.,
London and Exchange Streets, Norwich.
Notes of a Lesson on
24.10.20.
Day and Night.
Stds 3+4.
Time 30 mins
Aims. To prove to chn in a very simple way how day & night occur.
To train observation and to maintain interest throughout lesson.
Apparatus B.Bd, Chalk, Candle, matches, apple, knitting needle and globe & ball.
Introduction Chn will be told to imagine that they are in a dark room, with nothing to lighten it but a candle.
Secondly must think of the apple

as being circular like the tennis-ball.

Matter	Method
1. (a) The light from the candle only illuminates one-half of ball at once.	Chrn will then be asked what will happen if a ball is held near the flame (it will be illuminated) Elicit from chrn that the half nearest the light will be lit up, while the the half away from it will be dark.
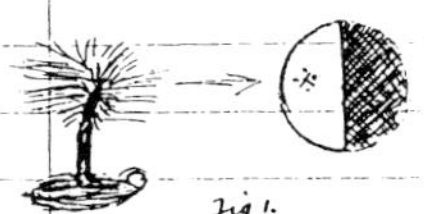 Fig 1.	Tr will shade in part marked * on ~~diagram~~ ball with white chalk. Fig 1.
(b) Methods of getting the dark parts illuminated	Elicit from chrn what they would do to let to light show on the other side of the ball. Perhaps they will

Matter	Method
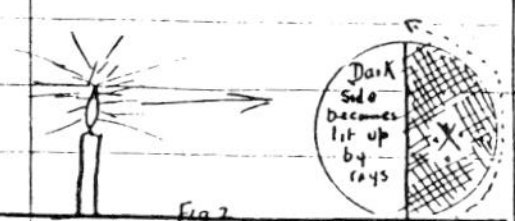 Fig 2 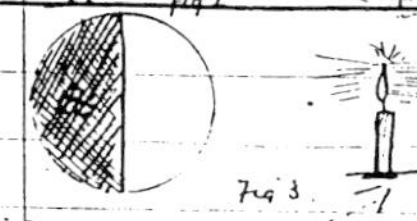 Fig 3.	say, "Turn the ~~the~~ chalked side of the ball round so that the other side is lit up; or, move the candle round to the other side of the ball. Figs 2 & 3, or thirdly,
(1) Move ball round light (2) Move light round ball. (3) Turn ball round.	move the ball round to the other side of the light. Thus chrn will see three methods of turning the dark portion into light & v. versa.
2 (a) The apple on the knitting needle can be taken in same manner.	Tr will next use the knitting needle and apple. A place will be marked with

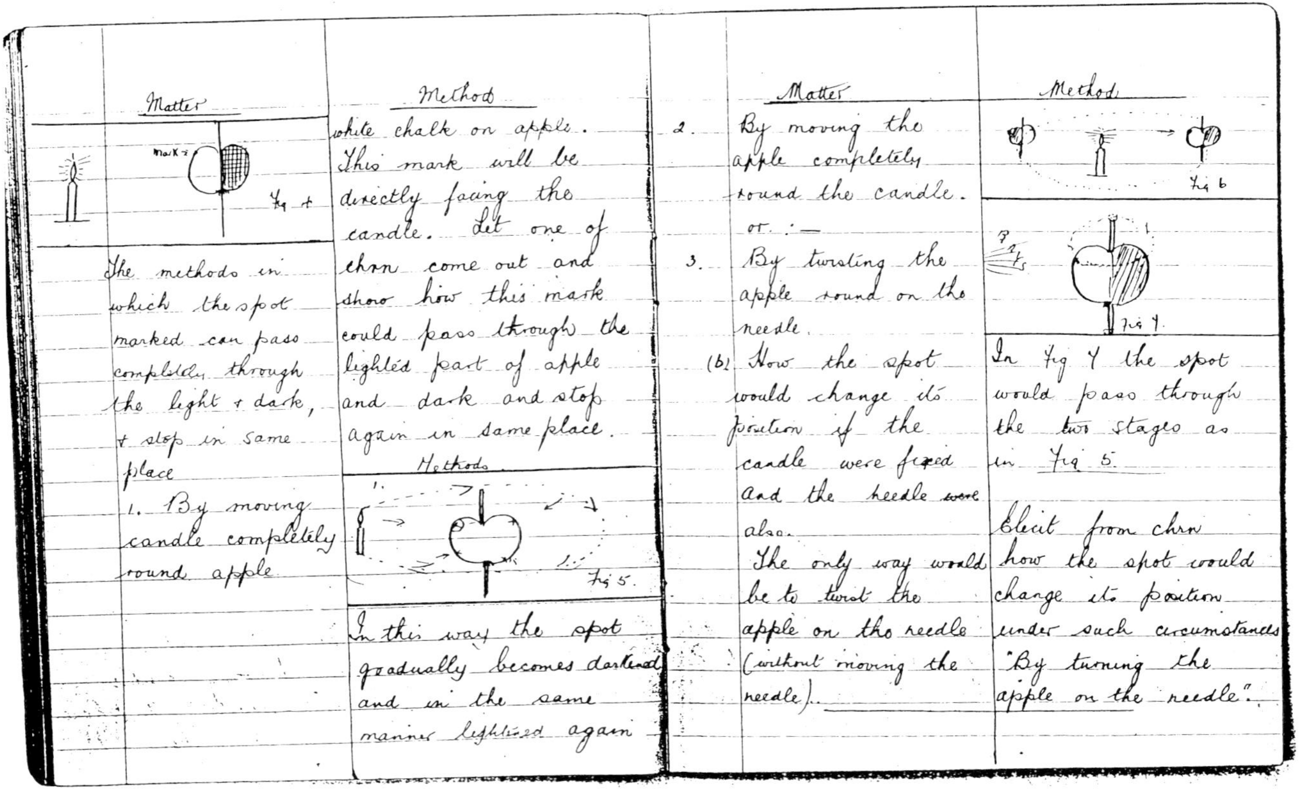

Matter	Method
Fig 4 (mark =)	white chalk on apple. This mark will be directly facing the candle. Let one of chrn come out and show how this mark could pass through the lighted part of apple and dark and stop again in same place.
The methods in which the spot marked can pass completely through the light + dark, + stop in same place	
1. By moving candle completely round apple	Methods (Fig 5.)
	In this way the spot gradually becomes darkened and in the same manner lightened again

	Matter	Method
2.	By moving the apple completely round the candle.	Fig 6
	or :—	
3.	By twisting the apple round on the needle.	Fig 7
(b)	How the spot would change its position if the candle were fixed and the needle also.	In Fig 7 the spot would pass through the two stages as in Fig 5.
	The only way would be to twist the apple on the needle (without moving the needle).	Elicit from chrn how the spot would change its position under such circumstances "By turning the apple on the needle".

Matter	Method
3. (a) The use of the candle ~~of~~ as the sun and the globe as the world.	Thirdly, let chrn see the globe - Ask them what the globe stands for and what it is lit up by. Tell them they are to imagine the candle as the sun shining on the world (the globe)
 Fig 8	Let one of chrn find our country on globe, then ask chrn which way our & land passes through the light and dark stages Does the sun pass round the earth? Does the earth pass round the sun?

Matter	Method
	or Does it turn round and round like the apple did on the knitting needle.?
(b) Chrn's seasons for thinking the sun goes round the earth.	Perhaps chrn will say the <u>sun</u> passes round the <u>earth</u>, and their season will be, that the sun seems to move because it rises in east and passes Vis. the S. to the West.
	Tr must make it clear to chrn that it is the earth moving and <u>not</u> the sun.
(c) Knowing the earth moves the	

	chrn. will see that when the & B. Isles face the sun they are having day & v.v.	Elicit from chrn why the people in Australia are having night when we have day.
4.	The earth's axis (illustrated by apple and knitting needle.	Perhaps chrn will wonder how the earth goes round and round. This can easily be illustrated by apple & needle. Tell them that just as the apple turns on the needle, the earth spins or rotates on it's axis
	Formation of Day and Night (24 hrs)	

B. B. S.

The sun does <u>not</u> move.
The earth turns on its axis.
It turns round every 24 hours.
axle = part on which wheel turns
axis = line on which earth turns

Criticism

A much improved attempt in every respect.
If same amount of interest is taken with all lessons much better results will accrue, than has been likely from one or two recent lessons.
Chief fault was that chn did not seem to understand earths axis.

Apparatus: pictures – maps – B.Bd. & chalk.

Introduction: Chrn. will see from map that there are countless lakes in Scotland – thus when asked questions concerning them will be able to answer. They, having already seen how few the rivers and numerous the mountains, will understand why lakes are so thickly scattered in the Highlands. [Mr. Ford has written 'Not clear' in the margin against this.]

The 'Matter' includes the following:

1. How a lake is formed – shown on B.Bd. by illustration – also how rivers rise in lakes.
2. Scottish Lochs: lakes – England; lochs – Scotland; loughs – Ireland.
3. Scenery.
4. Visitors & occupations. Loch Katrine is the most beautiful of Scottish lakes. Peasants [*sic*] get well paid to guide visitors or to take them about the lakes. Fishing as on the Norfolk Broads. Salmon, Trout.
5. Size & Names of lakes. Size – small compared with Swiss & Canadian Lakes. [Drawings of] Superior 350m x 200m – Geneva 38m x 14m – Lomond 24m x 8m [Katrine shown alongside as very tiny in comparison].Chief lakes: L. Lomond 24m long – L. Awe 23m – L. Ness – L. Tay – L. Leven.

Mr. Ford had this to say:

> Teacher's Language Tr. must guard against gram. errors. e.g. 'Which is the highest' – speaking of two lakes.
>
> Avoid continual use of 'now' (One sentence noticed 'Now think of a mountain now, now what etc') Don't ask questions admitting of 'Yes' or 'No' answers.
>
> Teacher's Manner etc. Tr. was earnest & anxious to impart plenty of information but was inclined to do too much & so leave chn. little to do. Questions are mainly too 'suggestive' – answers are almost 'put into chn's mouths'. Uses of lakes not mentioned.
>
> Lesson was well prepared. BBd map was good & BBd was well used for notes & sketches.

Joe's latent talents were obviously emerging here – the underlined words in the last sentence were to be stressed as being essential attributes of good teaching practice to countless students who came under Joe's wing in the years to come.

Standards 3 & 4 received a lesson on 'The Early History of Cape Colony' which Mr. Ford said –

> 'was well given & likely to produce good results. Chn. were very interested & answered well'.

It is followed by one on 'The Roman Invasion of Britain' – which is given no criticism for some reason – perhaps Mr. Ford was so impressed he was lost for words!

A 15 min. 'Physical Exercises' lesson, obviously modelled on the Army Drill Manual, was judged –

> 'A Good Lesson' but with the addendum – 'Always conclude lesson with short game or a few extra smart, quick movements. '<u>Jerk</u>' necessary sharp orders just a bit more. After single movements combine them e.g. 'Hips Firm, Rt. Foot Forw'd place'.
>
> (Signed) T. H. Ford
> 1/2/21

The 'Clouds' and how they are formed was introduced by 'show chrn. the kettle on the fire, as it is boiling, and ask them what they notice ....' At one stage in the lesson a red-hot poker was dipped into a beaker of cold water in order to produce steam and Joe offered the children the chance of winning a penny if they could do the 'trick' of getting it out of a saucer of water without getting their finger wet.

The headmaster warned Joe to –

> 'Be careful that chn's answers are strictly correct e.g. The "<u>kettle</u> boils"'. He goes on to say that 'Your ideas of steam & vapour are a bit mixed. Get this corrected & also correct it in chn's minds. Make chn. give their answers so everyone can hear. This will save you from having to repeat every answer given. Thoroughly thrash each little piece out before proceeding further.'
>
> Mr. Ford accepted that the 'Teacher endeavoured to make this a good lesson, but found it a most difficult task to make points clear, owing to laziness & lack of effort on part of children.'

These 'Criticism Lessons' were only a selection of the ones Joe was teaching at this time. He refers to a previous lesson, given by him to the class on the invasion of the 'Hardy Norsesmen', in his lesson notes for 'William the Conqueror', which he taught to

Standards 3 & 4 on the 15th February 1921. The notes indicate, judging by Joe's writing and the way they are set out, that they had been done the day before in rather a hurry and this is immediately picked up by Mr. Ford's first sentence –

> 'Notes: Not well written'. He goes on –
> 'Too much matter for half hour's lesson. This could have been made into two lessons.
> Teacher: Don't keep telling chn. what you are going to do e.g. 'I'll write it on the Blackboard'. 'I'll tell you'.
> Children: Most appeared interested but still a few made little or no attempt to answer. Several still seem afraid to speak out & their answers cannot be heard at all. * Encourage chn. to speak so all in class can hear.
> A F[airly] Good lesson, but Tr. should avoid trying to take too much in a short time. A little well done is better than a lot which is not fully understood. F.G. use was made of B.B. & some good questions were asked'.

Another 'Copy Writing' lesson. This example shows a vast improvement in Joe's own handwritten lesson notes. He could obviously do a perfect copperplate hand when he wished to!

> The Head 'noticed that several chn. were inattentive throughout lesson .... due to Tr. accepting simultaneous answers – the "dodgers" do nothing – a few work'.

Children never change!
This, the last lesson shown in the notebook, is signed and dated the 23rd February 1921.

Looking at the criticisms again it would be fair to say that Headmaster Ford was an astute mentor – he certainly 'spoke his mind' – but he passed on some very sound advice, advice which Joe made full use of in his own teaching career. At the time, when Joe was on the receiving end of these remarks, they must have bitten quite deeply into his consciousness and seemed fairly harsh. We have to admit that they were made of sterner stuff in those days! Five days a week teaching in the school all day, helping out daily in the family 'emporium' and in addition studying for his own examination, which he sat at the end of the four years. Small wonder he called it 'hard grind'.

Under the pupil-teacher system Joe would receive a small remuneration, perhaps a few shillings a week and be entitled to some extra tuition from his Headmaster but he was also obliged to travel twelve miles to Norwich every Saturday and attend lectures at the Pupil-Teacher Centre. Here, in the December of 1921, he sat the exam for what was known as the Cambridge Certificate and learned that he had passed on the 2nd February 1922.

The long 'practical' apprenticeship was over, but he had now to face yet another two years of training and this he undertook to do at The Diocesan Training College in York, under the watchful eyes of Principal, The Rev. H. Walker.

CHAPTER III

College Days as a Student 1922-1924

JOE HAVING CHOSEN TO continue his further education at St. John's College, York and being accepted as a student, arrived with his bags and baggage under the College portal in August 1922, aged 19 years.

Successive generations of students are always heard to say that the College isn't what it used to be in their day. Well, anyone looking at the College today would be hard pressed to even begin to imagine what it was like in 1922! In ethos, it was little short of being monastic and the buildings consisted only of the four wings enclosing the quadrangle, the Principal's house to the left of the front entrance and the Chapel facing it across the front garden. Tall cast-iron railings with two sets of imposing gates, set in massive stone pillars, enclosed the enclave from Lord Mayor's Walk and the small Victorian terrace houses of the 'Groves' crowded it in round the small open 'playing area' covered in cinders alongside the 'Model School' at the rear. Once inside there was no escape – and the Principal, the Rev. H. Walker (known to all as 'Taggy'), made sure of that!

Joe would be shown to his 'hutch', as the study/bedrooms were affectionately named, which consisted of a room about 10ft x 10ft with a bed, a locker and a desk and with one small window. It isn't known which corridor he lived on.

Very soon all the new students would be summoned to a meeting at which 'Taggy' issued the 'rules' of the establishment. 'You are not allowed to go out into the city after dark; certain streets – one of which is Coney Street – are out-of-bounds; No student must talk to any female outside College; you must not enter any public house or inn nor drink any intoxicating liquor; you must always be smartly dressed and on Sundays must wear a suit and hard felt hat' .... all of these and more on pain of being send down!

Joe seldom made mention of the daily rigours of College life but there are accounts written in *The White Rose* and the *Spread Eagle* by other contemporary old Johnsmen which give some flavour of life in College in the 1920's.

A typical day (Mondays to Fridays) read something like this:

7.30 a.m.	Roll Call
7.45 a.m.	Chapel – followed by Breakfast
8.30 a.m.	Drill/Exercise
9.10 a.m. to 12.40 p.m.	Lectures – followed by Lunch
2.05 to 3.05 p.m.	Lectures
4.00 p.m.	High Tea
4.30 to 6.25 p.m.	Lectures
7.30 p.m.	Chapel
8.00 p.m.	Dinner
8.30 to 9.00 p.m.	Private Study
9.10 p.m.	Roll Call
10. 00 p.m.	Lights Out

On Saturdays, students finished work at 12.40 p.m. after the morning lectures. Attendance at Chapel twice a day was obligatory every day of the week. All this was in theory but there have always been (and always will be) those students who make it their business to 'bend' the rules and there is no reason to believe that Joe was in any way exceptional! He was, of course, just a 'youngster' straight from school, albeit with four year's experience of pupil-teaching, but there were others who had served in the First World War who were rather more 'street wise' and not prepared to put up with all the traditional antics of the Senior Year nor the petty rules imposed by Principal Walker, as Albert James Copps 1919-21 (Enlisted in WWI 1915 – Demobilised 1919) pointed out:

> 'Who could forget that christening ceremony! On our first Sunday we had the use of the Senior study and we were issued with clay pipes filled with a vile mixture of stale tobacco, which we were bidden to light up and smoke during the fantastic rites. We older students had warned the organisers that we would not stand any indignities, so they had to moderate the forms somewhat. However we assented to the 'Sinjun' cross being made on our foreheads in a mixture of

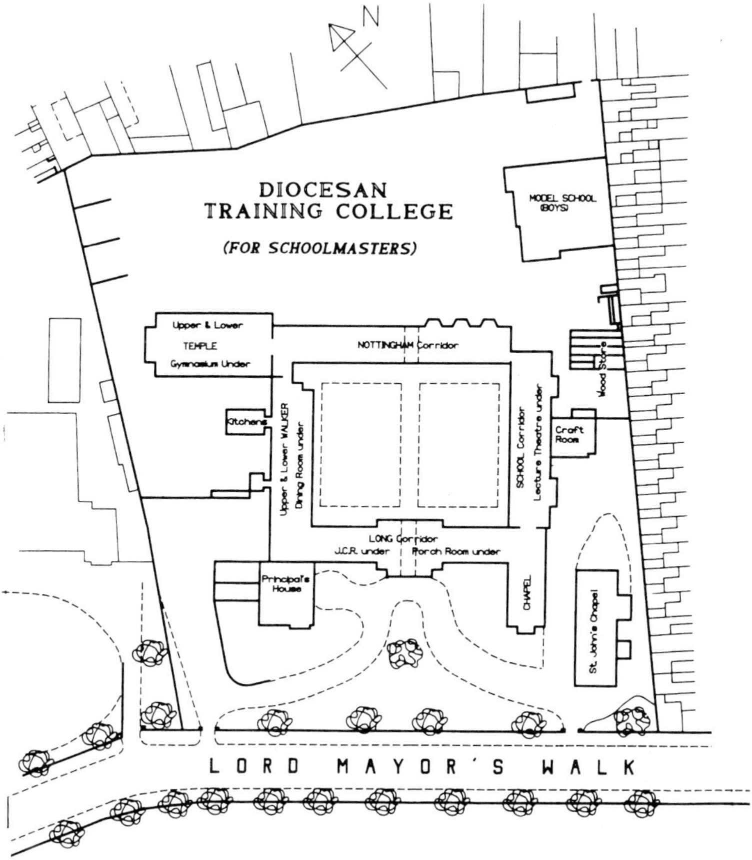

[© Drawn using CAD by Patrick Hunter]

Plan of St. John's College, York – 1930. Note barriers at both sides of building to stop the 'inmates' escaping!

whitewash, tobacco juice etc, as we were received into the noble order of St. John's (Sinjuns)'.

[In 1956 when I arrived at St. John's as a 'junior' there was still a vestige of this 'christening ceremony' being performed but only 'selected' students, picked out by the senior year students dressed as 'The Monks', were made to undergo some form of initiation. Those not selected were very relieved at not having to undergo this humiliation!]

Copps goes on to relate that –

> 'We were free most afternoons to disport ourselves, though Taggy was very watchful of our morals and put such areas as Coney Street out-of-bounds for some stupid reason. He was as sour and dour a specimen of the cloth as I have ever met. He had a protruding bottom lip that betokened a meanness of outlook. We had quite a job to reform him or to make him understand that we were not young lads but men who had come out of tribulations and having wives and families'.

Nor were the inmates very happy about the food they were being given and Copps records that on one occasion, at supper on Sunday evening, after being served with half a cup of watered milk and a ha'penny bun they struck.

> 'Taggy, the Vice-Principal and the other masters were sitting at the table on the dais, when we filed in to get our thick mugs half filled.... if there was sufficient in the ewer to accomplish this. Then after the hurried "Grace" we raised our mugs and let them crash on the table. There was a sound of smashing crockery, followed by a deadly silence, broken by the Principal's tensely uttered order, "You may go to your studies".'

Principal Walker is reported as having been furious and threatened to send everybody down for insubordination. After protracted negotiations with the students' chosen spokesmen Taggy was forced to give in but only after the students had said they would petition the Archbishop if they did not get better treatment. Copps concludes –

> 'Poor Taggy raved but our 8.00 p.m. "supper" became a late dinner that even exceeded our expectations'.
>
> Extracts from the *Spread Eagle* No. 16, 1973

So at least Joe, when he arrived at College a couple of years after this incident would have been provided with better nourishment than his predecessors although it is doubtful that as a growing young man he would get enough to satisfy his appetite. College 'tack' was often supplemented by food parcels from home even when I was at college and no doubt still is today!

One story relates that in the 1910's and 20's the students each had a small locker, at one end of the dining room, in which they kept a pot of jam or other little delicacy to supplement their rather plain meals or make them more palatable.

Another article recorded in the *Spread Eagle* No. 14, 1971, written by Allen D. Temple 1920-22 gives a similar 'feeling' to life in College during his stay there, just before Joe arrived. It is written in mock Biblical language and exhorts his 'Fellow Sinjuns' to attend the Fifty Years On reunion in College. One paragraph reads –

> 'Now it came to pass .... that the mighty king of the Sinjuns, who dwelt in the city of Ebor and whose name was Tag, sent forth messages to the uttermost parts of the land saying, "Thus saith the great king Tag, to ye which I have chosen; Ye shall now repair to the house of Coll, in the great city of Ebor. Tarry ye not but gird up your loins and bring what goods ye shall need and come. Ye shall sit at the feet of the great Tag and the feet of Fan and Willi and Budda and Jonah and Sloyd and the other great teachers that ye might also become scribes and disciples to preach the wisdom of Tag to the people in the uttermost parts of the land".'

Reading some of these tales told by old Johnsmen it appears that almost all students (as well as tutors) were 'christened' with a nick-name which ended in 'y' – hence 'Taggy' and later 'Fanny' Willmott and even later 'Prinny' Lamb, old traditions die hard. One wonders if Joe was known as Joey or Coppy – his middle name being Robert it could even have been Robby. Perhaps we may never know.

One of the things we do know about Joe's time in College was that he became well known for his outstanding blackboard work and it is said that 'Taggy' used to enlist his help in drawing the maps and summaries for most of his lectures.

Joe must have made a good impression on the Principal and the other tutors by the time he had completed his course as the references he received from them are referred to later in another reference written by his first headmaster at the Manor School, Mr. Teesdale. He records –

> 'The excellent reports on his character and ability received .... from the Tutors of the York Training College were well justified'.

The six long training years were at an end and Mr. Joseph R. Copping, now twenty-one years of age, was prepared and ready to go out into the world as a fully Certificated Teacher and, as we shall see or already know from subsequent history, to take it by storm in a most remarkable way.

CHAPTER IV

The Manor School 1924-1937

BEFORE JOE WENT DOWN from St. John's in the June of 1924 he had presumably been interviewed by the headmaster, Mr. M. G. Teesdale, and thus obtained a post as an assistant teacher at the Manor National School in York. The school took its name from the fact that it was originally housed in the King's Manor, having been opened in 1813 with places for 500 boys. In 1844, Infants and Girls departments were added 'under the boys school' within the Manor buildings. Instruction was given in English grammar, history, geography, with the elements of general history and mensuration being taught, but for an extra fee. An Inspection in 1850 found that no scripture was being read and that there were 9 classes in one room being taught **by one master and 6 pupil-teachers**. [Shades of Joe's 'apprenticeship'!] In 1922 the accommodation in the Manor was condemned and the boy's department moved into the former premises of the York Industrial School in Marygate which, until reorganisation in 1927 – as will be seen from a later entry – was rather a 'barn' of a place, where two or three classes were taught together in one room. At the time Joe joined the school the premises were still like this. There were about 220 pupils, all boys with a staff of six assistant masters plus the headmaster.

So, after what must have been a well deserved respite at the culmination of his six year training period, Joe returned to York and (according to the Manor School Log Book), on the 18th August 1924 'commenced duty as assistant master in charge of Standard V'. The log goes on to say that he 'has completed his training at St. John's College, York and is awaiting the results of the certificate examination'. He soon made his presence known as witnessed by the testimonial written by Mr. Teesdale in 1932 in which he says 'From the commencement of his service his outstanding ability has

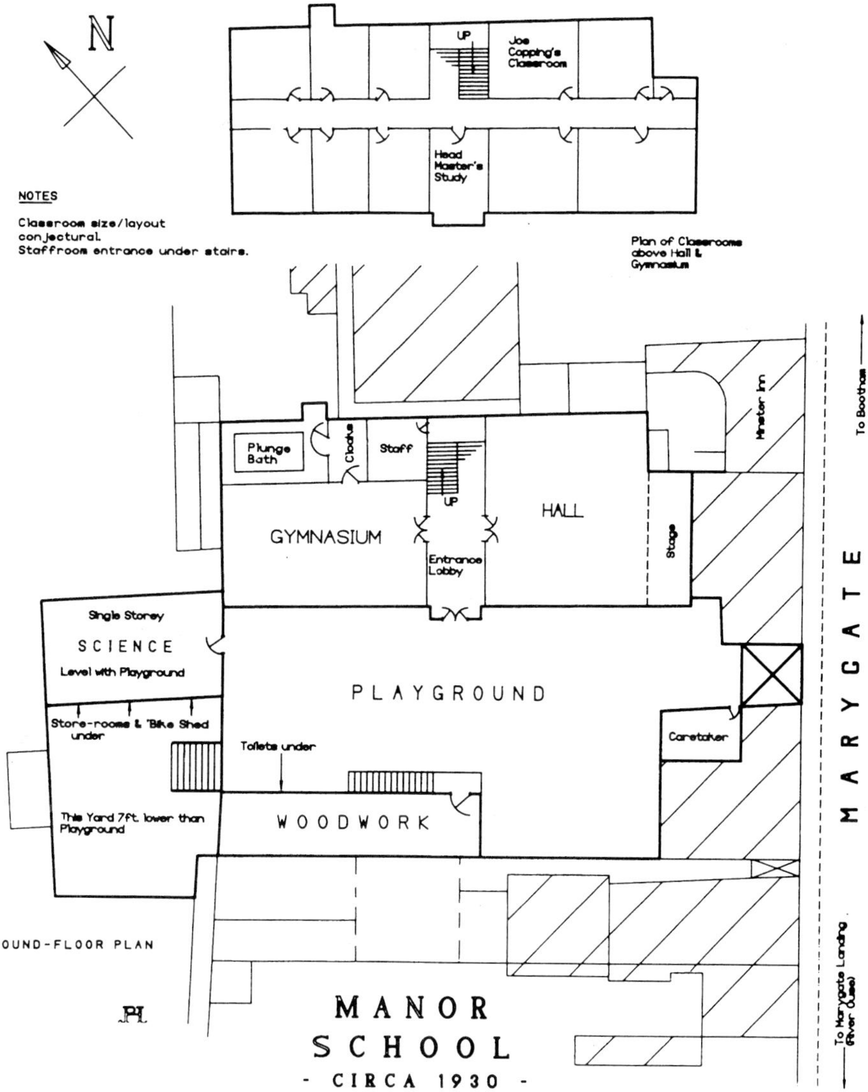

Plan of the Manor School in Marygate – 1920's.
Interior layout of main school building drawn from memories of former pupils – it may not be exactly to scale.

been apparent. His capacity for devoted and successful work, his rare initiative and enthusiasm, and his fine influence in the school quickly made him the most valued member of my staff'.

Extracts from the school log provide an indication of what Joe was doing during his early teaching career and no apology is made for quoting those entries which concern Joe in full, as they are recorded:

1924

August 28th: The headmaster with Mr. Copping's help conducted a Nature Study excursion (1.30-4.00 p.m.). Visited the River Foss and found much material for profitable study.

October 2nd: Headmaster assisted by Mr. Copping conducted an excursion to St. Mary's Abbey with Standard V. Purpose was to illustrate lessons on the monastic life and the dissolution of the monasteries.

October 20th: School re-opened after the October holidays and news was received of Joe's success in the certificate examinations. He obtained a mark of credit in Advanced Geography.

November 3rd: Mr. Copping was absent owing to illness.

November 10th: Mr. Copping returned to his duties.

December 23rd: Noted that attendance had been low during December owing to the outbreak of influenza. Standard V [Joe's Class] suffered seriously.

1925

During the winter months staff were encouraging boys to employ their leisure time profitably during the long winter's nights when they could not go out to play games. An exhibition was mounted in February. Standard V produced some excellent models illustrating the History course.

Registration Number of Mr. Joseph Robert Copping is 22/510.

May 28th: Mr. Copping conducted a Nature Study excursion with Standard V from 1.30-4.00 p.m.

September 15th: About 16 boys have qualified for the swimming medallions this season. Mr. Copping's regular and painstaking assistance with the teaching of swimming among the members of his class deserves special mention.

October 7th: Nature Study excursion with Standard V conducted by myself with help of Mr. Copping and Mr. Brogan.

December 14th: Mr. Copping received the sad news of his father's approaching death. He was absent from school from today having left for Norfolk and he will not return until after the Christmas holidays.

[Joe's father died on the 18th December 1925 at the age of 80. The epitaph on his grave stone in Worstead churchyard reads 'Absent from the body – Present with the Lord'.]

1926

January 11th: School re-opens and Mr. Copping resumed his duties.

REPORT OF HMI INSPECTORS carried out on January 23rd and 25th noted improvements in the new premises of Manor School on the site of York Industrial School. Previously large rooms containing 2 or 3 classes taught side by side. Now 10 classrooms – 2 still vacant. 5 classes have accommodation for 30 (pupils), 2 for 35 and 3 for 40 – total accommodation 404 but actually only 220 in attendance. 2 halls on ground floor. One used as an assembly hall and one a gymnasium. Present headmaster took charge when school moved to new premises and has been fully occupied helping it to regain the good reputation it had many years ago.

He gives class guidance to his staff especially the young and more inexperienced members who joined the school recently – demonstrated method in the classroom and developed discussions after school. Notes and suggestions were drawn up .... with a view to widening both outlook and interest. A good teacher Reference Library has been formed, a keen interest is shown in Nature Study and a school Museum has been established. Regular exhibitions of specimens are arranged so that they are easily accessible to the boys in one of the lower halls and frequent excursions to visit places of interest in connection with History lessons take place. Drawing in colour has been introduced with good results. Exhibitions of leisure work are held once a year.

May 27th: A Nature Study excursion was conducted by Mr. Copping with Standard 4A (2.50-4.00 p.m.).

December: Christmas entertainment consisted of selection of short plays, scenes and dramatised literature by individual classes.

Standard 4A – Mr. Copping's Class – presented a scene from *The Merchant of Venice* and also *Hiawatha's Photographing* (Lewis Carroll Ballet – an original production by Mr. Copping). All other classes produced one dramatic scene only.

[In an album of school photographs with explanatory notes added, in the possession of the writer, Joe has written the following under the heading 'OUR STAGE' –

> In 1925 we gave our various musical and dramatic items on the 'floor' of the Assembly Hall. In 1927 the boys planned and made a stage which can be erected in the Gymnasium, or in the playground on Speech Day. The costs of lighting, curtains and costumes were covered by the receipts of the concert given for two nights in 1928. Since then our annual Musical and Dramatic Entertainments have improved each year. For three years now we have 'sold out' for Wednesday, Thursday. & Friday performances.]

1927

May 5th: Headmaster re-appointed head of the Manor Higher Grade School.

[Under the reorganisation of the National Schools in 1927 Higher Grade Schools were introduced 'to give an academic education to the abler children in the senior elementary schools'. Besides the Manor there were seven other such schools established in York and all were fitted out with laboratories and woodwork rooms. In the entry above it will be noticed that the head was 're-appointed'. At the same time Joe's post was under consideration and it can be seen in the testimonial to Joe written by Mr. Teesdale in 1932 that the Head petitioned the authorities to ensure that Joe too retained his post at the 'new' school:

> 'So great was my confidence in his (Joe's) worth that, when the school was selected for re-organisation as a Higher Grade School in 1927, I eagerly requested the retention of his services in the more advanced work of Specialist Teacher in which he had proved so eminently successful'.

Joe was appointed Senior Geography master.]

May 19th: Mr. Copping conducted Nature Study excursion with Standard 4A (1.30-4.00).

June 24th: Standard 4A under Mr. Copping's direction produced two dramatic presentations of clever nonsense 'Pyramis and Thisbe' (from '*A Midsummer Night's Dream*') and 'The Mad Tea Party' (from '*Alice in Wonderland*').

June 29th: Party of 18 boys in the charge of Mr. Copping joined a large party of York children in a visit to Croft to see a TOTAL ECLIPSE OF THE SUN at about 6.30 a.m. Great disappointment – the sun was obscured by thick cloud but we saw gradual eclipse almost to point of totality. The train left for Croft Spa at 4.05.

August 22nd: School re-opened as a Higher Grade School.

November 8th: Mr. Copping absent from school owing to illness. Medical certificate received.

November 21st: Mr. Copping returned to duty.

December 20th: Part of the afternoon was devoted to dramatic presentations by 3 higher grade forms and Carol singing. Programme included a scene from the *Merchant of Venice*, a short play in French, a scene from Moliere in English, a recitation of poems in costume and other musical and dramatic items. Mr. Copping and Mr. Twilley [he was the French master. Ed.] were responsible for the entire programme and the result was very successful.

1928

May 7th: [Joe's Birthday. Ed.] Mr. Copping conducted an excursion with form 1C in connection with his Geography teaching.

May 10th: An excursion was conducted by Mr. Copping with form 1B to Clifton Ings. The low level of water gave an opportunity to study terrace formation, delta formation, alluvial flats and other geographical subjects.

1929

March 12th, 13th & 14th: Musical and dramatic entertainment performed in the gymnasium by boys of the school in aid of York Church School Fund. Parents and friends attended. Special audience on 14th – students of St. John's College. Mr. Copping's skillful production of the Shakespearean scenes was much appreciated.

Visit to the Gas Works conducted by Mr. Copping, Mr. Bell [Science master. Ed] and Mr. Twilley.

December19th: Dramatic entertainment between 3.00 and 4.00 p.m. Programme included scene from Shakespeare's *Taming of the Shrew*, produced by Mr. Copping.

1930

March 25th: The school lantern (*sic*) was used by Mr. Copping in giving special Geography lessons to some of his classes.

November 4th: Mr. Copping conducted 2 excursions in connection with his Geography teaching, 1B and 1C – 10.30-11.55 and 2.00-3.00.

November 18th: Programme of dramatic entertainment included the following items prepared by Mr. Copping – Scenes from *The Merchant of Venice*, 'The Fooling of Malvolio' – from *Twelfth Night* and *Hiawatha's Photographing* – a parody by Lewis Carroll.

1931

May 27th: Attendance for May 13th, 25th and 26th entered in error by Mr. Copping in register for form 4. Mr. Copping's eyesight is sometimes very uncertain particularly when he is not feeling too well.

June 1st: Excursion for geographical observation and sketches conducted by Mr. Copping with form 4 (1.30-2.50).

September 11th: Headteacher drew the attention of Mr. Copping to an error in his attendance register. 'I initialled and dated the error'.

November 27th: Winter swimming sessions commenced at St. George's Baths under Mr. Bell, Mr. Copping and Mr. Earp [Maths master. Ed.] who have volunteered to assist.

1932

March 10th: Annual exhibition of work done during leisure. Special interest shown in Geography as a result of Mr. Copping's enthusiasm and the number of note books on widely varied geographical subjects is large. The quality and usefulness of independent work is particularly apparent in the Geography section of the exhibition.

March 16th & 17th: Musical and dramatic entertainment was given by boys in the gymnasium, due to the willing and very able co-operation of Mr. Copping and Mr. Twilley.

May 26th: Mr. Copping conducted an excursion in connection with the Geography teaching of form 4 (elementary surveying from 1.30-4.00 p.m.).

May 30th: Mr. Copping who has in all his work displayed initiative, skill and devoted interest has instituted with much success a study table in the gymnasium at which boys may sit and read interesting works on Geography, enjoy illustrations and make notes from maps and literature. It is well used during leisure moments.

June 30th: Mr. M. G. Teesdale on doctor's and specialist's advice resigned his position as headmaster of this school due to a serious mental and physical breakdown.

[It was at this stage that Joe was appointed Temporary Acting-Headmaster for the ensuing four months. Joe must also have been applying for a Headmastership – the Testimonials reproduced below, written by Mr. Teesdale and by the Vicar of Worstead, reinforce this view as does the subsequent entry in the Log Book, for October 4th, which mentions an interview.]

Worstead Vicarage
Norwich
11th July 1932

Mr. Joseph Copping has been known to me for the past twenty years, and it gives me pleasure to testify in his favour.

He was a pupil and pupil-teacher in Worstead School, where his conduct was consistently exemplary and his work entirely satisfactory. Since he has been away from home I have, of course, seen less of him, and I am unable to speak of his work in York, but when we do meet he refers to it with enthusiastic interest, and does not regard education merely as a source of profit to himself.

Mr. Copping's home is in this parish and members of his family are well-known to me. I can confidently testify that he has had the advantage of the best moral influences, of which, I believe, he has always availed himself, as he has done with all his opportunities, and I conscientiously believe that his own influence would be advantageous to any pupils for whose welfare he was made responsible.

(Signed) C. W. Kershaw M.A. (Oxon)
Chairman of the Managers of Worstead School
Vicar of Worstead-with-Dilham, and
Rural Dean of Tunstead

CITY OF YORK EDUCATION COMMITTEE
The Manor – Higher Grade School – York
22nd July 1932

This school was very fortunate in securing eight years ago the highly efficient services of Mr. J. R. Copping as Assistant Master on the completion of his College Course. The excellent reports on his character and ability received at that time from the tutors of the York Training College were well justified, and the promise which he gave of unusual capacity as a teacher has been amply fulfilled.

From the commencement of his service his outstanding ability has been apparent. His capacity for devoted and successful work, his rare initiative and enthusiasm, and his fine influence in the school quickly made him the most valued member of my staff. So great was my confidence in his worth that, when the school was selected for reorganisation as a Higher Grade (i.e. Selective Central) School in 1927, I eagerly requested the retention of his services in the more advanced work of Specialist Teaching in which he has proved so eminently successful.

Mr. Copping is a teacher of exceptional resource and high ability. I know no teacher who possesses initiative and originality in so remarkable degree. He brings to his teaching a living interest which clearly indicates his own love of his work. Careful and inspired preparation of his lessons, sound and cleverly adapted method and conscientious thoroughness in teaching have combined to achieve the best results in the school. His success in cultural subjects is as remarkable as his varied ability in these subjects which form the solid essentials of primary education.

There is always an atmosphere of happy work in Mr. Copping's classroom. His boys respond readily to his pleasing personality, and to his well directed and purposeful efforts. Class-management is to him always easy, whatever the age of his pupils may be. His boys are unconsciously stimulated by his own high standard of work.

Mr. Copping has the advantage of careful preliminary training as a teacher in Norfolk, and his teaching experience at this school has been particularly valuable. He has taught a very varied range of subjects in both junior and senior classes. The problems which have naturally arisen during the transitional and experimental years of reorganisation have proved his unusual skill in organisation, his clear and accurate judgement, and his adaptability.

Prompted by keen interest in his boys and in the work of the school, Mr. Copping has always been the first to offer generous, unselfish, and loyal co-operation in general school activities. He has organised and supervised school games and athletic sports with great efficiency; he has devoted his leisure to the teaching of swimming; he has conducted school excursions and educational visits; much of the success of the school's annual exhibition of leisure-work has been due to his efforts; and the skilled presentation of plays which he has produced at the school have demonstrated his ability in dramatic work.

Mr. Copping's gentlemanly bearing, fine character, and high integrity have won the respect of his boys and of the Staff with whom he has worked so happily. The influence of deep spiritual sincerity has marked his religious teaching and extended through all his work to the boys who owe so much to him. I have long relied on him as the most able member of my Staff, and I am convinced that in his personal character, his exceptional ability, his skill in organisation, and in his tact and sympathy in dealing with young teachers and with pupils will be found all those qualities both personal and professional which are to be desired in a Head Master. I know no Teacher more worthy of promotion.

(Signed) M. G. Teesdale
Headmaster

1932 [*Cont.*]

October 4th: Mr. A. G. Bell and Mr. Copping attended an interview at 2.30 p.m.

1933

March 17th: Geography excursion. Form 2C with Mr. Copping – formation of soil and river erosion – 10.50-11.50 a.m. 1.30-4.00 p.m. Form 4 went to hilly fields near Bishopthorpe Road for surveying.

March 29th & 30th: Above excursions repeated.

September 29th: Form 4 with Mr. Copping visited the Mansion House 2.00-3.00 to inspect Civic Plate, also went into the Guildhall.

1934

January 20th: Mr. Copping took 10 boys to Scarcroft School at 3.30 to a concert given by a string orchestra.

February 10th: Mr. Copping took a party of boys to see *Twelfth Night* produced by the York Settlement Players.

July 12th: Talk with Mr. Copping and Mr. Herrell [P.T. & Geog. Ed.] on the Geography Scheme for 1934-35.

November 12th, 13th & 14th: Evening entertainment. Programme included short farce called 'Hoodwinked', written by Mr. Copping.

1935

February 11th: 38 boys visited the Rialto cinema with Mr. Copping to see *Wild Cargo*, a film about wild animal life in Ceylon and Malaya.

February 23rd: 20 boys went with Messrs Copping and Herrell to see the film *Through China and Japan* in connection with Geography.

June 6th: Third year boys went to the Railway Museum in connection with History teaching with Messrs Copping and Rutherford [History master. Ed.].

June 19th: Form 4 with Mr. Copping visited fields at Bishopthorpe for surveying.

[Mr. Jackson, the Headmaster, wrote the following appreciation of Joe.]

The Manor Higher Grade School
York
20th June 1935

Mr. J. R. Copping has been a member of the Staff of this School since August 1924.He has been Senior Geography Master since 1926, and has infused into the boys in his charge great keenness in this subject. In addition, Mr. Copping has had a wide experience throughout the School in teaching general form subjects.

Mr. Copping's work is stamped with thoroughness, showing great care in preparation, is presented with a high degree of proficiency, and obtains an immediate response from the boys in his charge.

As House Master of 'Stuart' House Mr. Copping has rendered great service to the school by his unremitting attention to duty in this respect and by the time which he has generously devoted to the out-of-school activities of his 'House'.

He has, too, a distinct flair for Dramatic Work, which has been an outstanding feature of the Annual School Concert.

He is a good disciplinarian, obtaining the attention of all boys, without the slightest friction.

A keen study group in Geography has been formed through the enthusiasm of Mr. Copping, and the work they have produced in their leisure time received the commendation of His Majesty's Inspectors.

For four months Mr. Copping was Acting Headmaster of this school, and carried out his work with great efficiency, to the entire satisfaction of the managers and the Education Committee.

I can recommend him with every confidence.

(Signed) G. F. Jackson, B.A. (Lond.)
Headmaster

1935 [*Cont.*]

June 21st: Form 2B with Mr. Copping visited river to study erosion.

July 10th: Mr. D. H. Cooper appointed headmaster.

September 1st: Mr. D. H. Cooper B.A. took up his duties as Headmaster.

October 9th: Four top classes with Messrs Copping, Rutherford and Netherwood [Maths and English master. Ed.] visited special lectures in connection with Health Week.

November 1st: Mr. Copping ill.

November 14th: Mr. Copping returned to duties.

November 28th: 58 Boys from 8 forms with Messrs Copping and Nicholson [Craft master. Ed.] and the Headmaster attended Robert Mayer's concert in the Exhibition Building. [In which the Art Gallery is now housed.]

December 10th to 13th: A musical and dramatical event was given in the Gymnasium on each evening. About 80 boys took part in the various activities – scene painting, costume making, singing, acting and programme production. The room was filled on each evening, more than £22 being taken. The Programme included:

1 Scenes from Shakespeare
2 Group singing Irish Songs
3 Sword Dancing
4 Solos and Recitations
5 'Poor Cinders' – a pantomime burlesque
6 'Songs of Seven Nations'
7 P.T. Display
8 'The Ashes' – a mime
9 Mississippi Minstrels

1936

January 6th: School re-opened with 247 boys.

[Once again Joe must have been looking for promotion to Headmaster. He was given the following reference by Mr. Cooper – the third Headmaster under whom he had served at the Manor School.]

The Manor School
Marygate
York
17th June 1936

Mr. J. R. Copping has been a member of the staff of this Selective Central School since August 1924, and Senior Assistant Master for a number of years.

He is a man of high academical attainments and I can honestly say that after long experience in many types of school, he is the greatest teacher that I have met. His lessons are most stimulating and the results are manifest and highly gratifying. He gains the complete devotion of his pupils; the brilliant ones are inspired to efforts that provide for their fullest development and the slower ones to discover in themselves powers previously neglected.

Mr. Copping is responsible for the organisation of Geography and Music throughout the School and his work has been the subject of very favourable comments, both verbal and written, by H.M. Inspectors. He acts as a House Master, undertakes the control of an efficient Prefect System, does a great deal of work necessary for the production of the School Magazine, and is responsible for the conduct of a highly successful Play Circle, which for the last seven years has produced plays annually in a highly meritorious manner. In order to make best use of Mr. Copping's undoubted gifts in this direction, I have recently re-organised the time-table in order that each Form may be under his supervision for dramatic work.

His work as a Senior master of the School has been excellent in every respect and I venture to predict that as a Headmaster he would prove a complete success. He possesses to a remarkable degree those qualities which a Board of Governors would look for in a candidate for a Headmastership – tact, courtesy, sound disciplinary power, striking teaching ability, unflagging zeal and industry and a high conscientiousness.

I write this testimonial regretfully as Mr. Copping's departure would be deplored by boys and masters, and would be a grievous loss to the school. Nevertheless, I feel that he deserves a Headmastership and would be an inspiration and a power for good in such a position. I wish him every success.

(Signed) D. H. Cooper, B.A.
Headmaster

1936 [*Cont.*]

October 13th: 25 boys in charge of Messrs Copping and Nicholson went to Robert Mayer's concert in the Exhibition Building at 2.30 p.m.

December 14th to 18th: On each of these five evenings a musical and dramatic entertainment was given in the Gymnasium which was full to capacity each evening. More than 80 boys took part and more than £27 was taken. The Programme:

1 Group of Japanese Songs
2 *Brother Sun* by Laurence Housman
3 'Songs of Seven Nations'
4 P.T. Display
5 Lantern Slides of School Activities
6 Pantomime – *Aladdin*

1937

February 23rd: Messrs Nicholson and Copping went to orchestral concert (3rd of Robert Mayer's series) at the Odeon Cinema.

July 30th: Manager's meeting held in Col. Scott's office, Mr. G. Herrell appointed vice [in place of. Ed.] Mr. Copping as Geography and Music teacher.

August 31st: Mr. J. R. Copping terminated his long and efficient period as assistant master at the Manor School to take up duties as lecturer at St. John's College.

As we close the Log Book, it may be of interest to know something of the colleagues who Joe worked with during his thirteen years at the Manor School. There were, of course, his three Headmasters already mentioned – M. G. Teesdale, G. F. Jackson and D. H. Cooper, the latter remaining as head at the Marygate premises until they were destroyed by enemy action in 1943.

'Jimmy' JAMES took Maths and played football for Norfolk. He followed Mr. Earp who had also taught Maths and had been the Housemaster of 'Abbey' (Yellow House); A. T. LEECH taught French and followed Mr. TWILLEY who taught the same

Staff of the Manor School – Circa 1936. Left to right, back row: 'Jimmy' James, A. T. Leech, Joe Netherwood, Evan Nixon, 'Gerry' Herrell, George Alderson. Front row: 'Tommy' Rutherford, Joe Copping, D. H. Cooper [Headmaster], 'Alf' Bell, Horace Nicholson.

language; Joe NETHERWOOD joined the staff in September 1932 when Joe Copping was Acting Headmaster. He came straight from St. John's and taught Maths and English. He later became Headmaster of Acomb Primary School; Evan NIXON – known as 'Tough Ted' took Maths; Gerry HERRELL (ex John's) taught P.T. and some Geography, later took over from Joe; George ALDERSON, who came from Swaledale and was ex John's, taught Art; 'Tommy' RUTHERFORD took History and later became Headmaster at Whixley. He was Housemaster of 'Wentworth' (Red House); 'Alf' BELL took Science and was later Headmaster of St. Paul's School in York. Also the Housemaster of 'Manor' (Green House); Horace NICHOLSON joined the Manor staff in 1927 and remained on it, after the school moved to the Priory Street Methodist School premises in 1943, until 1947 when he was appointed to Nunthorpe School. He taught Craft throughout his teaching career and during the war taught Woodwork to the ladies who were shortly to be engaged in constructing aircraft parts.

[A few years ago Mr. Nicholson kindly looked through some of the old Manor photographs I had been given by Joe. He identified the people on them and gave me some of the background information noted above. He died in December 1995.]

To finish off the list – Joe COPPING, Senior Assistant master, taught Geography and Music and among all his other duties and extra-curricula activities was Housemaster for 'Stuart House' (Blue).

It is not possible to include in this publication all the photographs in Joe's 'Manor School' album but the notes he appended to some of the pages make interesting reading and these can be included.

> 'SPORTSNAPS'. Many of the snaps in this album show teams of Manor School boys at the School's Sports or with trophies they have won. The boys had an amazing run of victories in all branches of sport, winning in 1933 the – Football League; Football 'Cup' Competition; Cricket League; Athletic Championship and Swimming Championship. This season a team has won the 'Daily Dispatch' Shield for Football in York.

Photographs show the teams who won the respective awards as well as boys practising gymnastic displays on a tennis lawn and displaying their skills on stage.

> 'SHAKESPEARE'. By the addition of incidental music, and the use of a black curtain at 'half' stage it has been possible to produce several plays in shortened form. 'Props' have been made by boys, and where necessary scenery has been painted by them. So far our productions include: '*The Taming of the Shrew*' – '*Julius Caesar*' – '*A Midsummer Night's Dream*' – '*Merchant of Venice*' and '*Twelfth Night*'.

The Photographs in the album include the 1929 and 1933 productions of *The Merchant of Venice*; the 1932 production of *A Midsummer Night's Dream* and that of *Twelfth Night*, given in 1931: *The Taming of the Shrew* was produced in 1934: Undated photographs include scenes from, *Hiawatha's Photographing*; *Morte d'Arthur*; 'French Play'; 'The Italian Museum'; 'Hoodwinked'; 'Choobs'; 'Johnnie Schmoker'; 'Coon Songs' (*sic*); 'Legend'; 'The Bishop's Candlesticks'; 'Songs of Seven Nations' and 'Japanese Songs'.

> 'ORIGINAL PLAYS'. Several short plays by members of the staff have been presented from time to time. These have usually been of humourous nature and include: 'Choobs' – a farce in a doctor's surgery; 'Jamaica Jem' – fun in a village

'stores' – 'Hoodwinked' – a roadside comedy and three playlets in French.

Other photographs show Joe's class of 1931, the School War Memorial [which the present Manor School Headmaster, Mr. Peter Smith, told me had 'gone missing' – if anyone knows where it is please let him know], and some examples of pupil's 'Leisure Work'.

In *A History of the Manor School* by Richard Evans (1987) it is quoted:

> In 1924 the House system is first mentioned as is school uniform, the wearing of which led the Headmaster to write, 'I am gratified to see that efforts to secure a neat and gentlemanly appearance amongst the boys are not unsuccessful'....
>
> .... The idea of education for leisure seems a relatively new one but in 1925 an annual Exhibition of Leisure Time Work was started. Drawings, pottery, raffia work, two sets of Wireless Apparatus and numerous Meccano models were on show and prizes worth two guineas were given....
>
> .... [In 1926] The third issue of the school magazine – the 'Manorian' – sold over 400 copies.

Although Joe is not mentioned by name in the 'History', some or all of the innovations mentioned above bear his hallmark and it is very interesting to note that they all took place shortly after he joined the Manor School staff.

So ends another 'chapter' in Joe's life – one which has certainly not been covered adequately in these pages – but who could record everything he managed to do?

Joe touched the lives of hundreds of students during his time at 'Manor' but it was no passing acquaintance, he is still remembered with respect and affection by those who were fortunate enough to have him as their teacher.

Quite by chance, on two separate occasions, I mentioned to two of my friends, Ken Horwell and Keith Jackson, that I was writing Joe's story. Both immediately said – 'Joe Copping? He taught me at Manor'. There then followed two long conversations about all they remembered about Joe, his lessons and his involvement in all the school's activities. Both men are in their seventies but their recollections of Joe are as fresh as if they had left school yesterday.

Amateur Dramatics. A Midsummer Night's Dream *(1932).*

Football and Athletics, Manor School (1933-34).

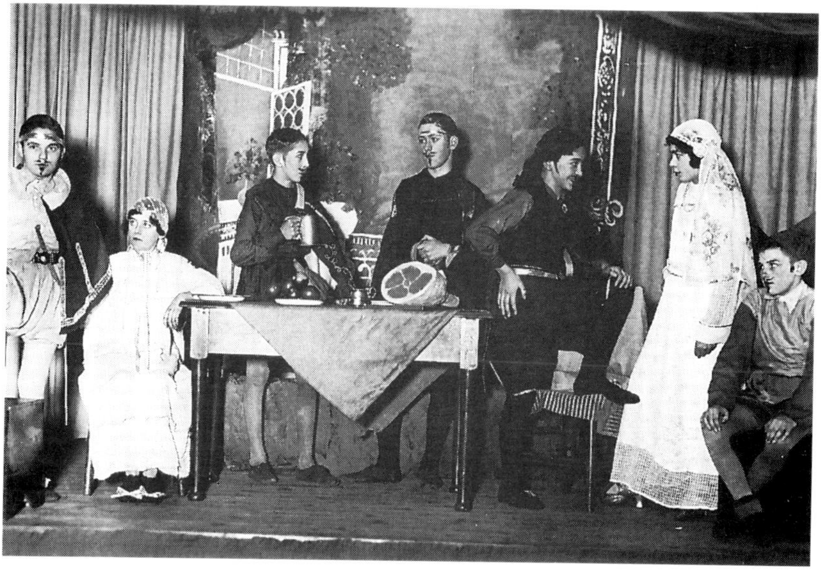

Amateur Dramatics. The Taming of the Shrew *(1934)*.

Songs of Seven Nations *(1935)*.

CHAPTER V

Intermission

THE THREE REFERENCES WRITTEN by three different Manor School Headmasters, Mr. Teesdale, Mr. Jackson and Mr. Cooper in 1932, 1935 and 1936 respectively indicate that Joe was seeking promotion to a Headmastership. All the Heads speak very highly of his abilities, skills and commitment to his calling and there is no doubt that Joe would indeed have made an excellent Headmaster. Only two instances of possible posts are indicated from the evidence I have found, those being for the Headship at Dunnington School and the other as 'Organiser' of the Day Continuation Classes run by Rowntree & Co. Ltd.

Reading between the lines it appears that, in the early part of 1937, Joe had approached Mr. Welch, the recently appointed Principal of St. John's, for a position in College but as the prospect of getting one was not certain at that time the Principal had recommended Joe to the Rev. H. M. Cooper the Vicar of Dunnington, whose letter reads as follows:

The Rectory
Dunnington – York
Telephone: Dunnington 49
5th February 1937

Dear Mr. Welch,

Many thanks for so kindly writing about Mr. Copping. He seems to be exactly the kind of man we need, for the School is certainly not in a very efficient state and we must have someone who will improve things.

Mr. Taylor does not retire until the end of July.

At present there are 115 children, but when the School becomes more efficient there could be an increase as some of the parents are sending their older children to York elementary schools. There are three certificated and one uncertificated teachers. The School buildings are all right. The house, the Hd. teacher lives in, does not belong to the School but is rented by the East Riding Ed. Committee. It is a poor house, but will sure to need some doing up and I think I can get the Education Committee to do this. I am a member of the County Council and when I am over at Beverley I will have a talk to the Clerk and perhaps the Chairman as well.

Perhaps, if Mr. Copping thinks favourably of the School, he will come and see me later on. We are only four miles from York.

Yours sincerely,

(Signed) H. M. Cooper

Whether or not Joe did think favourably of the school at Dunnington can only be deduced from the fact that he didn't become the Headmaster there.

The job at the Day Continuation Classes at Rowntrees was, however, offered to Joe after he had been for interview, but things were not quite straightforward, as can be seen from the letter following:

St. John's College, York
Telephone: 3596
THE PRINCIPAL

Dear Copping,

I find myself in a dilemma; I may be able to offer you a post here, but I cannot promise anything. If you came, I should have to do without the proposed Geography tutor, & before I could offer you anything I should have to get the permission of (a) the Board & (b) my Governors. The chances of you being offered a post here are good so far as my power is concerned. If you like to take a chance, then refuse the Day C. School; if you are not given a post here, you could stay at the Manor pending another H/M ship.

But the decision must be yours, & yours the responsibility. I can & do promise nothing. If you do go to the Day C. School, you will not be able to come here.

The decision about the post here will not be finally taken until the end of June. I shall leave here on Monday, so if you wish to see me again come in at 8.30 a.m. on Monday.

Yours sincerely,

(Signed) J. W. Welch
1.v.37

The Rev. James Welch.
The Principal of St. John's College (1935-1939) who appointed Mr. Copping to the Staff in 1937.

Joe now had to make his decision – he had already been offered the job at Rowntrees but there was the possibility of a post in College. What should he do? He acted very quickly after receiving the Principal's letter (and perhaps having seen him on the Monday morning), by penning a letter to Rowntree & Co. The following reply is dated the 4th May, three days after Dr. Welch's letter.

ROWNTREE
THE COCOA WORKS
YORK
Telephone: 2071
Ref: CHN/C 4th May 1937

Mr. J. R. Copping
The Manor School
Marygate
YORK

Dear Mr. Copping,

I am sorry to hear from you that you have after all decided to decline the offer of the post of organiser of the day continuation classes. Nevertheless, it was a pleasure to meet you and to give you any assistance towards making up your mind.

Yours sincerely,

(Signed) C. H. Northcott
Labour Manager
ROWNTREE & CO. LTD.

So the die had been cast and Joe had to wait and see what the Board and Governors of St. John's College made of his application. In the event it may be true to say that they made a very wise decision, one which countless Johnsmen and colleagues have, over the following twenty-six years and beyond, reason to be thankful for.

Mr. Copping was appointed Lecturer in Teaching Methods on the 1st September 1937 and began his duties on the first day of the Autumn term.

CHAPTER VI

St. John's College 1937-1963

Mr. Copping – The Tutor

THE REVEREND DR. J.W. WELCH M.A., M.Ed., Ph.D. had only nicely settled in as Principal having taken up his post just two years before Joe re-joined his old College, this time as a tutor. 'The winds of change' had blown the cobwebs of Principal 'Taggy' Walker's regime out of the dusty corridors of Long, Temple, Nottingham, School and Chapel and Joe was the first of a 'new breed' of tutors to be appointed by Dr. Welch. 'Fanny' Wilmott the Vice-Principal, C. R. ('Charlie') Wardle and J. Haworth would be known to Joe as former tutors during his sojourn in College as a student in 1922-24. Other members on the staff in 1937 were T. J. Wall, H. E. Inman, H. J. Davies J. D.('Dunc') Edington, J. ('Jimmy') E. Coleclough, and our 'old' friend Stanley Watkin.

The new Principal was intent on gathering together fresh tutors whose outlook would be more 'modern' and in line with his own radical thinking and he appointed The Rev. P. N. Wansey and J. Mackay at the same time as Joe. The Rev. 'Lenny' Poore and 'Jimmy' Shields soon followed, in Principal Cock's time, and Chris Chapman, Stanley ('Binny') Barnes, 'Jack' Edbrooke, Rev. O. T. Owen and Frank Disney were appointed by Principal Lamb. It is interesting to note that the 'y' ending of so many names is still evident.

Joe soon made his presence known, not only as a tutor of Education and later, Geography, Hygiene and Health Education, but as a most able organiser of social activities and 'developer' of the corporate life of the College. According to Principal Cock, writing in 1941 –

'Mr. Copping is in fact quite invaluable as a member of the staff of this College'. He also says of Joe .... 'He not only lectures in Methodology to our students, but he also gives demonstration lessons in a great many subjects ordinarily taught in schools and shows himself to be a teacher of imagination, inventiveness, resource and exceptional skill. He is untiring in his efforts to help individual students in the preparation and execution of their lessons.'

Legions of students will know how true these words are and it is quite impossible for one individual student to express the experiences of so many. All the writer can do is to echo all that has been said and written about Joe's extraordinary expertise as an educator of teachers and to remember with gratitude how, when standing in front of every class of pupils which I subsequently taught during my teaching career, Joe's 'words' and 'actions' were always at the back of my mind.

Looking at the 'Front and Back' book used by 'Primary Trained' students in all Joe's lectures brings to mind the methodical way in which he 'taught us to teach'. My own book begins with 'The Teacher's Personality' – which gives hints and advice on how to cultivate good relationships with pupils – followed by 'Some Important Rules of Classroom Technique'. Here are a few of them:

1. Stand back from the class. Try not to teach from the middle front desk.
2. Always use your eyes to advantage.
4. Have two blackboards if possible, one for a neat summary and one for incidental work.
6. Do not throw books at children.
9. Discourage walking out. Never have a queue waiting at the teacher's desk to be marked.
11. Cultivate the art of story telling.
13. Never be sarcastic.
16. The teacher's behaviour, attitude, conscientious effort and tidy appearance are reflected in his/her class.

Quote – Valentine Davies – 'Meticulous preparation is more than half the battle in teaching'.

Next came 'Blackboard Work' and 'Visual Education' with many examples of good work shown on cyclostyled sheets and others drawn by myself, obviously copied from examples Joe had drawn on the blackboard. And so it goes on through 'Correcting

St. John's College – Senior Year Students and Staff – Circa 1947.
Staff – seated second row – from left:
[Student] – H. E. Inman – Frank Disney – Jack Edbrook – Stanley J. Barnes – Miss Doris Pearson – J. D. (Dunc) Edington – F. A. N. (Fanny) Wilmott [Vice-Principal] – Principal P. J. Lamb – C. R. (Charlie) Wardle – J. E. (Jimmy) Coleclough – J. R. (Joe) Copping – J. B. (Jimmy) Shields – W. C. (Chris) Chapman – Rev. L. A. (Lenny) Poore – Stanley Watkin [Bursar] – [2 Students].

and Marking Children's Work', 'Dramatic Techniques', 'Speech Training', 'Specialisation' and 'Visits and Excursions'. The 'other' end of the book is concerned with critical appraisals of either actual lessons demonstrated by Joe or ones taught while students were on School Practice. Examples are given of how to prepare for School Practice, how to write Lesson Notes in various subjects and how to use 'film strips' and 'epidiascopes' in lessons. All good, practical advice which proved invaluable afterwards.

These were some of Joe's 'Points for School Practice' – Class is mine for a month. Progress, neatness of work, marking and behaviour of children are my affair. Class Teacher – Humility and give help ALWAYS – show interest in work already in progress – be tidy – accept adverse criticism with dignity – don't give open judgement on bad work (in first week). Teach FACTS. Criticise your own lesson afterwards.

In our second year we tackled such areas as 'The Psychological Characteristics of Children', teaching and testing Vocabulary, Comprehension and Reading, the latter delivered by Miss Precious, the then recently retired Headmistress of Park Grove School, (Joe always called her 'Puff' because of a habit of blowing out her cheeks!), 'The Backward Child' and 'The Learning Process', amongst many others. Considering that the hard-backed 'Front and Back' exercise book contains 200 pages, 89 of which are filled from one end and 82 from the other there is little wonder that Joe was well known as an 'active' and enthusiastic tutor!

Every year Joe wrote up a new lecture notebook for himself. There are three such books extant, one for 1961-62, one for 1962-64 and another undated. They each contain, in addition to a wealth of practical, 'no nonsense', advice on how to teach Primary children, his own plans for the demonstration lessons he gave in front of his students, to classes from Park Grove School, which are fully written up, complete with blackboard summaries and pictures.

There are 'quotations' from Plato, Socrates and Aristotle as well as from the latest authors writing about education – with his own succinct remarks added. Copies of the cyclostyled sheets he handed out to students are also included in his own books, one of which is headed, 'Vacation Work' – a double-sided A4 sheet of 'essential' reading and other tasks to do during the Summer holidays!

In one book is the record of an 'experiment' carried out in 1957 with an 'A' stream 10-year-old class to test children's power of recall. He conducted six different 'lessons' in which Listening, Seeing, Reading, and Doing were the main forms of learning. Five months later he 'tested' the children to find out what they remembered of these lessons and found that the 'Doing' lesson brought the best results; 'Seeing' ranked as next best with 'Listening' well down the list. Joe warns students that such experiments can be affected by the part played by the teacher and by the fact that every lesson did not include only the one activity. He was a great believer in children learning by 'doing' and this experiment proved that he was right.

It is interesting to note the 'differences' in Joe's notes for the 1960's to those we were given in the mid 50's. His 'Hints before School Practice' in the 1961-62 book contain these 'gems' –

> Stand erect – press your knees back. Have everything ready.
>
> Children can sense – Lack of confidence – Laziness in preparation – A 'don't care' attitude.
>
> They will give you hell (especially 7-9 age group) and you'll deserve it.
>
> Awkward pauses and breaks to 'write up' something which should have been on B.B. ask for bad behaviour.
>
> Without confidence, readiness and careful planning of notes you will rarely succeed.

Strong words coming from Joe, but were times changing and was he just keeping up with them?

Joe was at his best in helping students when it came to School Practice. His office at the back of the Porch Room, equipped with everything any self-respecting young teacher could possibly want, became a hive of activity. The 'Gestetner' duplicating machine never stopped whirring out cyclostyled sheets; students were shown how to cut stencils; 'old' stencils were held in front of the gas fire so that the backing sheets would peel off without tearing the skin; B.B.C. radio broadcast booklets were pored through for suitable pictures and card, chalk, pencils *et al* were procured.

Lesson notes had all to be signed by tutors before they could be taught in the schools and Joe saw students at 6.30 in the morning or at ten o'clock in the evening, if necessary, in order to get this done. He was always the first to offer advice if a student said he was having difficulty but was quite sharp with those who were slothful or arrogant.

When he visited schools to observe lessons you could be sure that his 'criticisms' were helpful and constructive and many a student has been given extra help and advice if Joe thought they were 'struggling'.

All Joe's students have their own special memories of him as their tutor but in all cases it appears that his approach was the same – teaching by example and by demonstration, not by merely lecturing, i.e. 'talking'. He practiced what he preached and encouraged students to become involved with doing practical work with the children. The results were seen annually in the Porch Room Primary exhibitions which are described elsewhere under the heading, 'Joseph Copping – The Organiser'.

This is what Ronald Wells (1941-43), writing in *The White Rose* of 1991, has to say about life in College during the war and about Joe.

> 'I first set foot in St. John's College in September 1941 to embark on my professional studies course for Junior and Senior teaching, as they were designated at that time.... This was war time and the small number of Johnsmen had been added to by a contingent of those who in happier times would have been pursuing their studies at St. Bede's, Durham. After the Baedeker raids of April 1942 students from St. Luke's, Exeter and Saltley College, Birmingham were also evacuated to St. John's. The first air-raid on York occurred a day or two after our return from the Easter vacation and we had just been on our preliminary visit to the schools allocated for the second Teaching Practice....
>
> I look back on my studies as being of very high quality in spite of the problems, which were fully matched by the unswerving dedication of the lecturing staff in "keeping the show going" during those difficult and hazardous times.
>
> It does no disservice whatever to the others to make special mention of Mr. J. R. Copping who became a legend in his own lifetime for his quite outstanding contribution not only to the development of our professionalism but also to the social life of the College. In spite of the tragic loss of his wife and unborn child in the first air-raid (we were stunned and mystified by the apparent injustice), his strong Christian beliefs sustained him. He returned to his professional responsibilities and redoubled his efforts setting an incomparable

The War Years.
Principal, Professor A. A. Cock with the College Cadet Corps.
Joe Copping – Front row, second from the left.

and unforgettable example to many. His was the driving force behind the concerts, the Saturday evening dances and much else, and as Secretary of the Music Circle I can personally testify to the creative energy he invested in all these activities.

It was his inspiration, his untiring resolve to transmit to novices like ourselves as much as possible of his own remarkable classroom expertise and the patience and skill with which he discussed and re-shaped our halting, stumbling efforts at lesson design and preparation must have become the basis of our own educational philosophy and professionalism.' [extract only Ed.]

But, 'Joe the Tutor', at which he was exceedingly gifted, was only one facet of the life of this extraordinary polymath. Had it not been so then this account of his time at College could be brought to a conclusion at this point and the fascinating story of his involvement with the 'life' and 'soul' of the College and of the students who studied in it, could remain untold.

Joe Copping – The Dance King

I will let Joe tell his own story to begin this section. This piece was written by him and published in '*The Spread Eagle*' No 13 in 1970.

COLLEGE DANCES

I am not sure whether this article should be called Evolution or Revolution.

My experience of dances at St. John's dates back to 1922, when, infrequently on Saturday evenings, we were allowed to make 'Mild Whoopee' in the Art Room. Sandwiched between Chapel and Roll Call (7.30-9.10 p.m.) we danced in P.T. gear and indulged in a programme of country dances, lancers and old-time progressives to piano accompaniment. Under the discerning eye of Charles Wardle the dances were strictly unisex. No female was allowed to enter the monastic portals. Some of you reading this will remember the famous threat, 'We don't want you pushing prams down Gillygate'.

With the arrival of Dr. Welch there came a social revolution and more frequent dances were arranged in the Dining Hall. Staff and students appeared in lounge suits and usually introduced their partners to the Principal and Mrs. Welch. Student dance-bands provided the music for fox-trot, quickstep, waltz and various old-time medleys. By 1937 the Charleston was in the decline. The first Archbishop's Night Dance in the gymnasium was a great success and included at half-time a pantomime.

Then came the war and like the Windmill Theatre 'we never closed'. I remember Professor Cock saying 'Joseph, the social life of the college must go on' and the gym windows were painted black, and shuttered. For over five years we had weekly dances, and very frequent concerts and variety performance in the lecture theatre on Sunday evenings. Students too young for call-up arrived from Bede, Cheltenham and Saltley and with the fifty Johnsmen left at college, donned gay-coloured blazers for our Saturday dances. At this time partners were invited weekly by post, and the Social Committee were kept very busy. Hitler was kind to us, for not once on a Saturday evening did we have an air-raid warning in York. Adversity bred a very close companionship and we forgot the hard times, to the strains of Glenn Miller, Harry Roy and Joe Loss. 'Charity' Dances were frequent in the war years and our most successful was for 'Mrs. Churchill's Aid to Russia' (at the time of Stalingrad) when we raised £106 at a Saturday 'do'.

In 1946 came several changes and some college dances reached their peak in popularity. We decided to have season-tickets for our lady friends. The energetic Social Committee compiled a list of ninety reputable young ladies (hopefully over 16) and added their friends as time went on. I suggested that these ladies should come in free and the men pay a 1/- instead of 6d (today 7s/6d is a frequent charge!) I kept this important list, which soon became known as 'Joe's Marriage Market' (and there are many happy Johnsmen today with their Saturday Dance Wives!).

A new amplifier with two speakers added zest and volume to our programmes, too loud for some (I remember Mrs. Lamb enquiring politely whether there was a volume control). We moved into the Geography Department and the ladies (much to Ron Smith's delight?) used his domain as a powder room. On one occasion a pair of silk stockings was found in the map drawer. It was here (in the New Wing) that we managed ingenious decorations (especially on Club Nights) when sports clubs and college societies organised the events. The end wall was reserved for my B.B.S. programmes. About this time the Principal [Canon Lamb. Ed.] suggested that the Archbishop's Dance should move to the more elegant and spacious Assembly Rooms, where the Assembly Players provided an excellent programme for £18. (Pop Groups today ask £70.) In the early fifties we started our Learners' Classes. For the first three sessions each September students had the opportunity of learning to dance. Mrs. Shields helped me demonstrate the steps, and here we were fortunate in having a few students who had diplomas in ballroom dancing. May I take this opportunity of thanking them once again, and all the keen members of our Social Committee.

During the fifties arrived Rock 'n Roll which at first we called 'Swingstep' and later 'Jive'. Bill Haley and Elvis Presley caused some to flinch but many to revel in the new rhythm and din. I must confess that I liked the novelty. The 'Dashing White Sergeant' was not yet dislodged! The Principal excelled in this vigorous gallop. But Victor Sylvestor was on his way out – he'd had his day (and so had I).

One day in 1963 Christopher Chapman called me across the quad, 'Come and hear this record I've just bought'. I went. It was the Beatle's first record to 'sell a million' entitled '*From Me to You*'. From that day dancing has never been the same.

There is very little that can be added to Joe's account except to admit to being one of his 'Marriage Market' 'victims'(!) – no, that is not the right word – I am indeed a very happily married (old) Johnsman with two grown-up children.

Judith, my wife, was one of Joe's 'season ticket' holders and first went to the College dances in 1957 – during my second year. At that time the young ladies all wore 'flouncing' layers of net waist-petticoats under their dresses and they made a fine show when they swirled around the dance floor. 'Prinny' was one of the most enthusiastic onlookers – when Helen wasn't around!

I was operating the gramophone at that time and remember how Joe always arranged the records in 'threes' for each dance. Then, there was a short break so that the men could take the ladies back to their seats. This gave everyone the chance to 'change partners', as indeed we always did, seldom dancing with the same girl for more than a couple of dances during the evening. If any of the girls were 'sitting out' Joe would soon find some shy student to dance with them or do so himself. 'Go and dance with that girl over there' he would say. 'Can't do it!', may come the reply. 'You never will be able to if you don't try! – Come onto the floor and I'll show you!' It was no good protesting when Joe was around – you danced.

There was always some tactical manoeuvring towards the end of the evening to make sure you danced the last waltz with the girl you intended to take home and a story is told that one newly-arrived student 'chatted-up' Mrs. Marion Shields, wife of the 'Senior' Education tutor, with a view to walking her home to The Limes! Happy days.

Mr. and Mrs. J. R. Copping

And that leads me to another very poignant phrase in Joe's article about the dances – 'Hitler was very kind to us'....

Hitler, or at least one of his airmen, dealt Joe personally a very 'unkind' blow.

In the December of 1937, just after Joe had taken up his post at College, he married a young lady by the name of Marjorie, seven years his junior, at the Parish Church of St. Olave in Marygate. At

Mrs. Marjorie Copping.

the time Marjorie lived with her mother and father, April and Caleb Oakley, in Lumley Road, Clifton. The marriage certificate dated 18th December is signed by the bride's father and mother, by Joe's ex-headmaster, David Harold Cooper and by the officiating vicar, the Rev. Francis Morse Windley. [Incidentally, the latter was also Chairman of Governors at the Manor School.]

Joe and Marjorie set up home at number 3, Fairway in Rawcliffe Lane and, if we read the reference written by Professor Cock on the 30th May 1941 (*ibid*), can see that he wrote at the end.... 'Mr. Copping has a most charming wife who very ably seconds his social work for our students'.

The happily married couple had been together for just under four-and-a-half years when, on that cruel night of the 28th April 1942, the German Luftwaffe Baedeker Raid on York extinguished the life of Joe's wife and their unborn child and left him seriously injured. A bomb had fallen directly down the chimney of No. 3 and then exploded, demolishing the house and that next door where Marjorie's brother lived. He too was killed and brother and sister lie together in an unmarked grave in Fulford cemetery. Students from the College helped to dig Joe out of the rubble and bring him back to Principal Cock's house where he remained for some considerable time.

Hitler was kind to us?

Joe's strong Christian faith together with the loving care and attention of Principal Cock and his housekeeper, Lottie, brought him through his ordeal and I am sure that he 'worked off' his grief by throwing himself even more into the life of the College by organising all kinds of extra social and cultural activities for the benefit of the students. 'They' had become his lost wife and child and 'they' would receive not only his skilled tuition but his love and affection for generations to come.

Marjorie's photograph always occupied a prominent position in Joe's room – he very, very seldom mentioned her to the students but I noticed during the years I knew him, that on the anniversary of her death he placed the photograph face down on the cabinet and for a couple of days I felt he was not 'his usual exuberant self'. Chris Chapman, the Vice-Principal, told me that on these occasions Joe always kept a low profile and went to sit quietly with him in his room on Long Corridor.

Thus did Joe live with his grief, but he very rarely let it show outside the close circle of his immediate friends.

A Change of Principal

In the September of 1939 Professor Albert A. Cock took up his appointment as the new Principal. The students (and perhaps the staff) were rather disappointed to be losing Principal Welch so soon and were keen to maintain the benefits he had brought to the College. They wrote in *The White Rose*.... 'We hope that the coming Principal will maintain the same happy relationship with the students'.

Whether this had anything to do with Joe looking round for another post in 1941 may never be known but the 'new' Principal wrote him the following glowing testimonial:

ST. JOHN'S COLLEGE, YORK
Telephone 3596
THE PRINCIPAL The Rev. Professor A. A. COCK
30th May 1941

I have much pleasure in supporting the candidature of Mr. J. R. Copping, Lecturer in Education and Music at this Training College, for the post which he is now seeking.

Mr. Copping who has been on the staff of this College for the past five years served his early years in teaching at Worstead, Norfolk, and he was trained at this College during 1922-24. After going down from College he had twelve or thirteen years' experience at the Manor School, York specialising in Geography, Music and English, but the reputation which he had deservedly acquired as a student at College and which was enhanced by his splendid service at the Manor School, York was such that my predecessor, the Rev. Dr. J. W. Welch seized the first opportunity to bring Mr. Copping on to the staff of the College in order that his quite exceptional gifts as a teacher and demonstrator might be placed for the benefit of successive generations of students.

Since I took up the office as Principal of this College in September 1939, I have myself had abundant opportunities of realising the very unusual versatility and gifts of Mr. Copping. He not only lectures in Methodology to our students, but he also gives demonstration lessons in a great many subjects ordinarily taught in schools and shows himself to be a teacher of imagination, inventiveness, resource and exceptional skill. He is untiring in his efforts to help individual students in the preparation and execution of their lessons. He has organised long distance visits to schools and important educational centres, e.g. to the Village College in Cambridgeshire, and his readiness to serve and his ability to adapt himself are so marked that he has lectured very effectively in Geography, Hygiene and Health Education. Since I came here he has also undertaken the larger part of the music instruction of this College, and the dramatic work of our students owes almost everything to his genius and unselfish devotion. He has also been a most able organiser of our social activities and despite the many handicaps imposed upon us by the war he has developed the corporate life of the College to a remarkable degree.

Upon the foundation of the St. John's College Boys' Club I asked Mr. Copping to undertake the dramatic work for this very large and flourishing youth organisation and he has done so again with marked successes. Mr. Copping's services have also been repeatedly used when training schools have been organised at this College for deacons and young clergy and once again his skill and sympathy have been of inestimable benefit to recently ordained men.

Mr. Copping is in fact quite invaluable as a member of the staff of this College and I feel very strongly that he deserves preferment to a much more important post than is at present open to him here and I recommend him with gratitude, pride and confidence to the notice of any appointing body. If he were given charge of a new school he would stamp it at once with the marks of his own delightful personality, originality and resource. Everyone taught by him would be stimulated, everyone who worked with him would be proud and happy to be on his staff. I should be very glad indeed to answer any question on his behalf. I ought to add that Mr. Copping has a most charming wife who very ably seconds his social work for our students.

(Signed) Albert A. Cock
Principal, St. John's College, York
Fellow of King's College London
Formerly Vice-Principal and Professor of Education
and Philosophy, University College, Southampton

Joe Copping – The Impresario

Where does one start to give an account of the myriad presentations Joe Copping created over a period of almost thirty years? I suppose it could be said that a start has already been made by outlining those he produced at the Manor School during the previous thirteen years and which in a way paved the way for the ones he masterminded in College. In the early days and throughout the war years Joe arranged musical entertainments, which took place on Sunday evenings, and introduced the regular Saturday evening dances with 'real' ladies as partners – something unheard of within the College precincts previously.

Joe was a master of 'Variety' – short sketches written and produced by him – normally with plenty of humourous content. Students with little or no acting ability were encouraged by Joe to take part and, after getting a taste of showmanship often went on to tackle more testing roles in his full-length plays. He made full use of 'twin' students and wrote sketches which played on their lookalike character. Tutors were often the butt of satirical nonsense and 'Lenny' Poore was even known to have lent students, who were 'taking him off', his hearing aid and dog collar! Often Joe appeared in the sketches himself. Two memorable performances which the writer witnessed were portrayals of Fagin in '*Pick-a-Pocket*' and as Noel Coward, resplendent in dressing gown and with cigarette in holder, performing '*Don't Put Your Daughter on the Stage Mrs. Worthington*'.

In 1947 Joe was the President of the Dramatic Society, and the Music Circle as well as being Chairman of the Entertainments Committee, all roles he fulfilled with equal zest. Extracts from *The White Rose* magazine illustrate the diversity and vitality of Mr. Copping's involvement with the social life of St. John's.

> DRAMATIC SOCIETY: 'Our *piece de resistance* was the production of *The Tempest*, which was cast from the senior year, giving much scope to all the talents of the actors and providing Mr. Copping with much food for thought and an outlet for his ingenuity'. In the same year '*When We Are Married*' by J. B. Priestley and '*Thread of Scarlet*' a one act play by J. J. Bell were performed and a play reading group formed so that the junior year could gain experience. The report ends with .... 'Finally, we wish to thank Mr. Copping

for his leadership and guidance and also for his unlimited patience displayed whilst directing our efforts'.

MUSIC CIRCLE: 'Our weekly programmes held each Sunday at 7.15 have proved exceedingly popular again this year. Audiences of over a hundred have been the rule....' .... 'A Series called "Themes to Remember", two Quiz programmes, a Musical Journey and "English Verse and Music" have added variety to our gramophone nights'.... 'We heartily thank Mr. Copping for his tireless efforts which alone have really ensured our continued success'.

ENTERTAINMENTS COMMITTEE: 'Our Chairman, Mr. Copping is a never-ending source of encouragement and the flow of ideas he has for novel and amusing variety items is an inspiration to us all'.

The Dramatic Society's *piece de resistance*, '*The Tempest*' is reviewed in the same edition of *The White Rose* as being 'a memorable production'. 'In Mr. Copping the play found an expert and discerning and sympathetic producer who was able to weld the actors into a team and inspire them to rise to the height of Shakespeare's great argument in this his poetic testament. As a result we were given no merely conventional interpretation of the play, but one with many skillful and delicate touches....'

In 1948 the Rev. Leonard Poore once again wrote the 'Criticism of College Performance', this time on the *Housemaster* by Ian Hay. He begins by saying that 'It is not easy for a college dramatic society to give a convincing performance of a play where some of the chief characters are schoolboys and elderly schoolmasters. However thanks to the careful and intelligent direction of Mr. Copping and the high standard of acting .... that willing suspension of disbelief for the moment which constitutes poetic faith was never once endangered'.

Much Ado About Nothing was produced by Joe in 1950 which was said to 'fully deserve the excellent reception it received from crowded houses on four occasions'. He was thanked by the reviewer 'for yet another successful production'.

In 1952 the 'theatre' was undergoing structural alterations so the Variety show produced by Joe was given in the Model School. This was not the first time that shows had been put on in other parts of the buildings. When, in 1938, Joe began to organise 'entertainments' at College the first 'bi-sexual' dances were held in the

Junior Common Room now the Alcuin Room. The Music Circles and early Variety Shows were also held in this room. The Dances and Variety acts were originally held in the Dining Room or the Lecture Theatre and later in the Senior Study Room on New wing.

During the war years a 'Cinema' was set up in the gymnasium which entailed 'blacking out' the windows with paint and shutters. These in-house movies proved to be very popular with both living-in staff and students and continued until the end of hostilities. The main Lecture Theatre was also given the same black-out treatment as the gym so that evening shows could continue to be given. The original seating capacity of this room was quite limited and the alterations mentioned above greatly enhanced it by extending at the back and adding a gallery above the tiered seats. After the improvements had been made the entire student body of that time could be seated in this room.

[As an aside, we who lived in School and Nottingham corridors used to use the flat roof of this extension as a sun-bathing area during the 'hot' months of the year – more often than not when we were 'clogging' for exams. Access was through a fairly high sash window at the end of School and many a time some joker would shut and lock the window so that those outside couldn't get back in and so were made late for lectures!]

But to return to the Model School Variety in '52. 'Record mimes', 'Oriental Mysteries' and the 'Sinjun Cads' were followed by Mr. Copping and E. Darlington in a new version of *Il Travatore*. Mr. Baggaley opened the evening by introducing the audience to Ravel and the closing item was given by the St. John's Singers.

In the June of the same year – now in the 'new' enlarged and refurbished theatre – Mr. Poore compered the show 'as deftly and wittily as ever'. Highlights were 'Eskimo School Prac', 'Ballerina Darlington and her all-star company', a double act by the twins W. & T. Hall – 'As in a Mirror', 'The Arts Council' and 'Esau's Escalator'. The latter said to be referenced to 'a recent dramatic production within (College) walls'. [Could it possibly have been Principal Lamb's *Go Down, Moses?* Ed.]

1954 saw a show which 'For sauciness, skill, originality and variety .... was unique'. 'Murder at the Co-op', 'A Bench in the Park' and 'Danger, Men at Work' were just some of the items offered. Once more Joe was the man who made it all happen and the reviewer ends by saying: 'Finally one must sincerely thank the producer, Mr. Copping, and those who helped behind the scenes, whose resource and energy made this show possible and not only a success but The Success'.

The following year under the heading of 'Variety' *The White Rose* report says that 'the programme.... was distinguished by its cleverness and wit and good humour'. It goes on – 'Outstanding were two items of burlesque and satire, both written by Mr. Copping, "The Wailing Women of Scunthorpe" – inspired by the College production "*Murder in the Cathedral*", and "Children of Genius" – a palpable hit at Modern Art. Worthy of comparison with these were "Melodrama" and "Woo-manship", the latter being especially notable for its telling impersonation of the Vice-Principal [Mr. Christopher Chapman] by Mr. A. Dixon'.

It continues to list over a dozen more items, amongst them being, 'Seeing Double' by Mr. Cherry and the Firminger Twins, xylophone playing, songs, mimes and solos. 'Item followed item without pause .... and made the programme go with a swing.' The review, by 'Lenny' Poore, ends – 'All who contributed to this Variety – and there are many – are to be congratulated on a "jolly good show" and not least the Producer-in-Chief, Mr. J. R. Copping'.

In that same year '*Murder in the Cathedral*' (T. S.Eliot) and '*I Killed the Count*' (Alec Coppel) were performed in College, the latter show produced by Joe. 'As we have come to expect of Mr. Copping's productions, the action moved quickly' is a remark made in the review and I can vouch for the 'slickness' of his shows having seen Joe during rehearsals. 'Come along now – the audience will have gone home by the time you make your entrance!' .... '**Snap** your words out as though you meant them' .... 'Stage hands – all those props must disappear off the stage in less than 10 seconds' .... and so he went on in quick-fire mode. Neither actors nor 'props men' nor anyone else connected with the show could be anything less than 100% 'awake' all the time Joe was around – nearly always in his dressing gown and with a Craven A on his lips. (That is if it wasn't during one of the hundreds of times that he'd 'given up smoking!')

The accolades continue to flood in for this remarkable man's productions, right up to his retirement in 1963 and even after that when he started to produce 'The Croft Socials'. How did he keep up the pace, the originality and the enthusiasm? It is true that over the many years spent in College he repeated some of the 'titles' of the plays and variety turns – but they were never the same. I have seen him glance through an 'old' script and then promptly begin to write it out again 'from scratch' with a new twist here, something added there, pieces taken out somewhere else until a completely 'new' script was created. Joe always kept up-to-date and so the appeal of his productions was always fresh and in tune with the current generation of students. His 'ideas' for Variety turns came from many sources; a snippet from a professional show he had seen, something that had happened in College, the presence of twin students, 'skits' on other more serious shows given in-house or on tutors, students' special talents or idiosyncrasies and so on. His ability to turn these into sharp, witty items was one of his special talents as was his knack of 'moulding' a bunch of amateurs into an almost professional team of actors.

These personal sentiments are borne out by Mr. J. C. Maycocks' words in his review of Variety, 1956. 'Attempts by amateurs to achieve the slick effects of the professional variety stage usually fail because of shortage of original material or because they lack the essential technical polish. The entertainment presented in College .... has no such shortcomings; the whole show was full of fresh, skillfully devised material, and moved at a brisk pace from beginning to end. Mr. Copping, who produced with his usual skill and energy, has welded together a large cast – sixty-four in all – and had them working as a team. This year's cast presented certain possibilities not always present – a real orchestra, some unusually good mime-actors, a pair of twins – and these were fully exploited.'

Mimes included 'Low Dive' – shades of a shabby cafe at closing time, 'In a Mirror' – well co-ordinated miming by the Firminger twins, 'The Impertinent Gloves' – with stage trickery – and 'West of Suez', said to be a glimpse of some colourful local customs vaguely familiar to some members of the audience! Spoken sketches included 'Mistake on a Balcony', a rip-roaring Victorian Melodrama and a serious little play on an Old Testament theme. Burlesque scenes called 'Exploded Myths' played gentle ridicule on old favourites like Davy Crockett, Christopher Robin and the old ballad 'Take thou this rose....'

Some serious items gave balance to the programme with a violin solo, songs and some magic tricks. The review ends with: 'A long programme with so many performers might easily have sagged in the middle, but it says much for Mr. Copping's direction and the team-work of the whole cast that the quickfire tempo was kept going throughout'.

The full-length plays presented in 1957 and 1958, *Sons of Adam* (written by Principal Lamb), *The Merchant of Venice*, *The Playboy of the Western World* and *Macbeth* were produced by Mrs. Helen Lamb and Mr. Maycock and Joe's involvement with these was mainly concerned with the back-stage management and make-up.

There was an epidemic of 'Asian Flu' in 1957, mainly affecting the new intake of students, and Joe was heavily involved with organising teams of second year students as 'nurses' and 'food waiters'. The sick bay could not cope with the numbers involved and those students affected with the illness had to remain in their own rooms. Joe painted large red 'plague' crosses on the doors of the afflicted and meals and medication were delivered to these rooms by the 'fit' students. As a consequence the main Variety show Joe had planned for this year had to be abandoned, but many of the prepared 'turns' were presented as part of the 'Floor Shows' at 'Club Night' Dances. At regular intervals during the year the various college clubs ran the dance; the blackboards were covered with drawings appropriate (roughly speaking!) to the club's activity, other decorations were strung across the room and a Cabaret at half time was provided. Students had to pay 1s/6d to attend these dances and the extra money was often given to a charity.

It would have been untypical of Joe had he been 'idle' in the way of providing some special entertainment for 'the troops' during the year and the following account is of an event in which he was heavily involved both 'up front' and 'behind the scenes'.

Formal Opening of the Music-Practice Rooms

Tuesday, June 26th, [1957] will long be remembered by those who were present when Lady Bucher arrived to open the new practice rooms for pianists. All who assembled were suspicious. Had not the President of the J.C.R. fooled us once already, when, on the occasion of the Marbles Tournament, a Lady Marfleet turned out to be Jack Tweddle in disguise? We did not trust Arthur Mitchell a second time.

Lady Bucher – or someone posing as Lady Bucher – arrived in a luxury shooting-brake dead on 7.30 p.m. The President and Mr.

Copping met her at the front entrance. 'Twasn't Tweddle again! Could it be Dyer? What remarkable make-up and what a perfect wig! (but was it a wig?) Whoever it was she (he?) met several V.I.P's in the porch then, preceded by Trumpeter Crewe and four gowned ushers holding gilt violin stands before them, she passed down the centre path. The Ad Hoc Poet Laureate of the occasion, Mr. Moody, carrying an impressively large roll of brown wrapping paper and flanked by Messrs Etherington and Stevens, brought up the rear with other dignitaries, all more or less academically garbed. Flash-photographer Morris and Trumpeter Crewe were close by at every turn as the crocodile made for the corner of Lower Temple.

It was a unique auditorium at three levels and in five directions. Mr. Copping introduced Lady Bucher to a peculiarly suspicious gathering arranged as in queues outside a cinema. To the left, right, above and round the corner they waited for another hoax. Was it Trees? Couldn't be Judd – he was an usher.

Mr. Copping told the peculiarly-arranged motley that Lady B's family came over with the Conqueror and opened practice huts for harpists; and that she herself had recently unlocked a new Skiffle Emporium in Las Vegas. But what made her so eminently fitted for the ceremony that was about to take place was the curious fact that she had just returned from the Congo, where it had been her proud duty to open practice rooms for Pygmies. (They sit cross-legged, leaning forward.)

Then Lady Bucher spoke, so that all could hear, even on Upper Temple. After a few words all realised that Mitchell had 'had' us again. This was a genuine, much-travelled lady, full of amusing anecdote and of fearless presence (she expected tomatoes). She was obviously enjoying the occasion.

Amid loud applause Lady Bucher and Mr. Copping donned crash-helmets and, armed with D.D.T. spray [*sic*], mounted the stairs to Little Baggaley (a small wing off Upper Temple). There, after ceremoniously opening six doors, they sprayed 'Mavis' (practice room No. 1) and 'Irene' (practice room No. 2), with a shot for luck on the Lower Temple assembly.

The helmets having been removed (and one or two unbelievers still waiting for the wig to come off), Mr. Copping read a telegram from the Vice-Principal, temporarily detained on the wrong side of the Pennines: 'Best wishes to all and two hundred and forty-six rockets'. The Rev. L. A. Poore then thanked Lady

Bucher for her kindness in coming, congratulated her on her dexterity with the spray-gun and presented her with a large dish made in our own Pottery department. He spoke with the oratory of Mark Antony and the vehemence of St. Paul. The drift of his argument was not always easy to follow but out of a splendid welter of literary and scriptural allusions emerged his unshakeable conviction that the new practice rooms were unique; no other educational establishment had ever possessed, now possessed, nor could at any future time ever possess such music practice rooms.

Mr. Moody now stepped forward, unfurled his scroll and fished out of his pocket a small piece of paper on which was written his 'Ode on an Auspicious Occasion.' In melancholy tones he read:

Let us to the sound of fife and muffled drum
Sing of the dreadful sufferings to come,
Sing of the music students pale and lean,
In the embrace of Mavis and Irene.

Sing of them staggering forth, broken in limb and head,
Off to the tender care of Matron's sick-bay bed.
Sing ye of claustrophobia and eke of suffocation,
Flattened skulls and twisted bones and excessive perspiration.

Sing ye, O sing ye of these sufferings to come.
Sing ye to the sound of fife and muffled drum.
But ere ye go, I pray ye, for the love of Heaven deposit
A tear in each melodious, mournful, maniac, padded closet.

Professor Judd of Cromer, concealed in 'Mavis' with a radio-gram and Rock 'n Roll record, now sought to prove that she was sound-proof. She was – almost. The proceedings closed with the singing of a new verse to the College Song. The Rev. Leonard having already practised his Beethoven on Little Baggaley, the addition is: 'Who will bump his bloomin' head?'

NOTE for future historians: Two charming and attractive young ladies, known to their friends as Mavis and Irene, assist the Bursar. They share his office and his generous sense of humour.

This report is not signed so 'future historians' may never know who wrote it but the writer, who witnessed the whole Lady Bucher affair, can confirm that it is indeed an accurate report.

In 1959 Joe produced Philip King's *Without the Prince* – 'an assured and happy production of an unpretentious comedy [which was] a complete success'.

The next year's Revue, 'Chestnuts and New Wine' – 'provided food for laughter if not for thought, especially on the first night. The second performance was slightly more slick and professional and rather more decorously received'. Items included 'A Shack in Oklahoma', 'Child of the Welfare State', 'The Bavarian Singers', 'Jabberwocky', 'Monks, Ancient and Modern' and 'Pick-a-Pocket'.

[Two incidents evidently added to the 'interest' (and suspense) of the show; one when an actor stood on an actresses skirt – ....'the show and the skirt were held up for some time....' and the other when a shoulder strap wouldn't stay in its proper place.] These account for the wording of the final paragraph of the report – 'No accident, however, was the success of the show; Mr. Copping was the inspiration of everyone concerned. His own appearances in "Pick-a-Pocket" and the finale, "Fings", were a fitting climax to a very enjoyable evening's entertainment. We can only hope that he has further delights for us in the near future'.

By this time Joe was preparing for his 'retirement' and handed over the Presidency of the Entertainments Committee to Mr. G. S. Smith, he himself taking the Vice-President's post for the last two years. He encouraged the students to take more responsibility for the production of the Revues and, as it turned out, was wise to do so as the next report confirms.

'Sunday Night at the Monkhouse', the 1962 Revue, was seen through by the deputy-producer, James Burchill, due to illness 'which struck Mr. Copping during rehearsals and also several performers on the day' [of the performance]. The report says that 'the show was predominantly musical'.

So the time had come for Joe to hand over the baton and the Entertainments Committee notes record that, 'It is with regret that we are losing one of our most active members this year. Mr. Copping in many ways has been responsible for the high tone of the dances, and it is with deep regret that we have to say goodbye to a faithful and conscientious worker'.

'Fings' would not be quite the same again in College – at least for a number of years.

Joseph Copping – The Organiser

I must now, of necessity, take the reader back in time so that we can look at yet another aspect of Joe's character, that of an 'organiser'. True, he could not have produced the many Variety and Stage shows he did without being an able 'organiser' but this section looks at the way Joe organised his own life and ensured that his department's Open Day displays and excursions, both events which were 'on show' to the public, went smoothly.

First and foremost Joe organised his own life to the nth degree – he was not one to say 'do as I say, not as I do' – he taught by example. He never wasted his own 'time' and detested 'time wasters' and any activity which he considered 'a waste of time'. He rose early and was often late to bed. I remember that sometimes after College dances he would invite a few of the 'helpers' back to his room in New for a cup of tea and a biscuit. As soon as it was his 'bedtime' he took off his shoes, said 'Good night everyone' and disappeared into his bedroom next door. That was it! Everyone took their leave of each other and went their separate ways leaving Joe to either go to sleep or re-emerge into the empty room to work – we never quite knew which!

His days in College were always full; lecturing, organising the next dance or show, always ready to help students, especially at School Practice time when he took up residence in the office behind the Porch Room and provided everyone who asked with what was required. He spent hours checking and signing Lesson Notes, often late into the evening, writing up his own lecture notes and countless letters to relatives and friends – many of whom were old students. In everything he undertook, meticulous 'preparation' notes were first written and re-written until he was satisfied that all would 'be right on the night'. As those who went on the 'famous' Leroy coach tours and other holidays with Joe will vouch, the entire schedule was worked out, discussed and written out in great detail before he even set off. Hotels, shows, travel arrangements, excursions *et al* were all booked in advance and once at the destination the days and evenings were a whirl of activity – he wanted to see and do everything that was possible (and often impossible) within the time allotted. Some of his companions who had rather less stamina than Joe, had often to cry 'pax' and take time off from his 'schedule' to relax and recuperate.

But most will look back on Joe's organisational skills and abilities in connection with the Educational Visits, to such places as Hutton-le-Hole and Pickering, with pupils from Park Grove School, students and other members of staff. With Open Day Displays and Christmas Carol Concerts in the Porch Room and with Dances, both in and out of College. I will let the several reports printed in *The White Rose* take up the story of some of these events:

OPEN DAY 1955: June 4th – 'one of the wettest days of the month'.

> 'In the Primary Department both children's and student's work could be seen and inspected, ranging from simple sheets of neat handwriting to a large frieze depicting the Middle Ages and covering one wall of the Porch Room. Model Theatres, felt, wire and paper animals, clay and tray models, and an enviable collection of cleverly-made puppets were to be seen, as well as the vacation and course work of the Department's second year students. The treat of the afternoon was a short but delightful show given by a few top-class children from Park Grove Primary School, who confidently and eagerly presented us with a musical band item and two cleverly-conceived sketches in a puppet theatre.'

OPEN DAY 1956: 'Dark clouds threatened rain the whole day .... but we must be thankful that it wasn't typical English garden-party weather – pouring with rain'.

> 'The Primary Exhibition was, as always, one of the highlights of the days' events and the Porch Room took on an atmosphere all its own, drawing crowds of admiring visitors during the afternoon.
>
> The Art and Craft section showed some of the interesting work that had been done with children earlier in the term. The balsa-wood 'planes and ships seemed exceptionally well made and there were also some clever lino-cut designs and paper sculpture.
>
> The School Practice table was a feature of the exhibition. Here was seen some of the outstanding work executed by students and pupils during the past College year, most notable of which was a Norman Castle.
>
> The nature table for May made a splendid contrast to all this, with its aquarium of fish, tadpoles and other water

creatures a predominant centre-piece, surrounded by many plants and flowers in their various stages of growth.

> The puppets once again intrigued the young visitors and amused the others. They were displayed in front of a theatre set of *The Sorcerer's Apprentice* and looked gay and cheerful in their bright costumes.
>
> Some very good Art work was displayed across the back wall of the room; particularly outstanding were the 'Poems in Pictures' done by the visiting class from Park Grove School. There were some delightful friezes, among which was a large and colourful one of the Norman Conquest.
>
> On one table was displayed useful visual material for Arithmetic, and on another one was some activity work in Scripture, which had been made by students of the second year. Basketry, craft and practical work in Nature study was also on show and there were some interesting accounts of recent school trips that students had made.'

Although there are no accounts of Primary School Excursions in the 1955 or 1956 editions of *The White Rose*, that of 1957 states that 'We had a fine day, the first for this annual outing in six years'. The writer could be accused of being biased in describing, in full, the account of this particular year's excursion as he has fond memories of taking part in it as well as being party to helping Joe with the production of the cyclostyled 'quiz booklet' which every student and pupil took with them on the trip. The account of the day was written by Joe – I have added a little.

> 'On Monday 24th June a party of thirty-four first-year students, four tutors and Standard IVA from Park Grove Primary School set off at 9.30 a.m. for a day's excursion to Pickering and Goathland. Every member of the party was 'armed' with a coloured map of the route, a quiz for the outward journey, plans (with keys) of Pickering Castle and Church and apparatus for Geography, Nature Study and Art at Goathland.'

The quiz questions began as soon as the coaches left the City boundary and kept everyone busily engaged during the entire journey looking for the answers. One I remember, near Goathland, was – 'We pass under one, over one and by one' – the answer being 'Bridges'.

'Visibility was good so that the view from the Keep of Pickering Castle was magnificent. We sat on the grass near the drawbridge over which eight kings of England are said to have passed. The children closed their eyes and tried to image a scene over six hundred years ago when Edward II visited the Earl of Lancaster and enjoyed hunting expeditions from the castle at Pickering.'

The story Joe told when we all had our eyes closed was sheer 'magic'. He wove a tapestry of fairytale-like splendour, The King with his couriers, all clad in magnificent clothes, galloping into the courtyard, the Castle Steward and the retainers scurrying around to welcome them, escorting everyone to their rooms in the great Keep, the kitchen hands carrying a sumptuous meal across the courtyard into the banqueting hall, the minstrels playing and singing round the hugh central fire .... and much, much more. When eyes were opened one wondered why all the buildings were in ruins and where all the people had gone. Joe was indeed a truly magical story-teller.

'At the famous old church the children were told the story of St. Christopher and were able to recognise several of the frescoes.

In spite of the ravenous sheep which seemed determined to climb into the boot of Bus 1 and demolish our pies, we enjoyed lunch at the foot of the Goathland Moors. In the afternoon some of the children with parties of students did some 'on the spot' Geography. Mr. Smith proved that configuration, contours and gradients present no difficulty when work is both practical and enjoyable. The study of flowers, trees and pond life was under the direction of Mr. Adams and the children were at the age when love of collecting and pressing, and of learning new names, had an immediate appeal.

After tea in a garden at Goathland and a romp on the moors we returned to York where, at nearly 7 o'clock, matron and the domestic staff welcomed us with an attractive and appetising supper.

One of the children has since written on behalf of the class: 'We had a lovely day. I enjoyed it all especially the food, but I wish we had been able to stay longer at Pickering castle'. To the child with a vivid imagination it seems that ruins can speak'.

J.R.C.

Such events do not just 'happen' as many readers will know, they entail a great deal of pre-planning, preparation and organising, not only beforehand but throughout the day. Joe's abilities as an organiser always ensured that all he undertook went like 'clockwork'. The old adage 'Whatever is worth doing, is worth doing well' – printed on the cover of his 'Criticism Lessons' exercise book of 1920 – must have made a lasting impression on his mind and he certainly lived up to it.

The Open Day in 1958 was graced by the Lord Mayor of York and the Sheriff and his Lady and once again the weather was reported to be 'dull'.

Highlights of the Primary Education Department's exhibition included 'a Saxon Village, a lighthouse, puppets, a group study called "The Romance of Bridges", an Elizabethan theatre, an aquarium, a television studio and programme for which the children had prepared scripts, the Haxby Road Marionettes, a scale model of 4th C. Eboracum a project on Fourth Milestone Farm, a tape-recording of a play written by children of Park Grove School, a study of cotton cultivation and processing and a project on the Yorkshire Ouse'. Not bad for a terms work!

The excursion again followed a similar format to the one already described – Joe's story at Pickering Castle this year including a 'horror story' of prisoners left to die in the 'forgetting chamber' and the brief imprisonment of King Richard II in the castle.

The quiz sheet is described by Joe as a 'blessing' – 'so much more restful than a "spouting" courier!' [He must have had to suffer many of these on his trips abroad. Ed.] 'The excited children watch keenly for six miles for a certain signpost – and then miss it. But for the most part they succeed in noting gradients of hills, the crops, the flowers by the roadside and the position of the villages on the map.'

Because of a cloudburst – with hail – shortly before they arrived at Goathland, lunch had to be eaten in the bus 'which can be a nightmare, but somehow we managed to balance pie, eggs, pop and apple tart on our knees. The Goathland sheep were most disappointed. Tea at the farm had [also] to be cancelled and in place of the proposed studies we rode to Whitby, over the moors to Scarborough and home, stopping only once for ices and a breather'.

The 1959 excursion report begins: 'For the first time for many years we had perfect weather'.

'Once again we visited Pickering and Goathland, which somehow have a greater appeal to the children than Lastingham and Hutton-le-hole.' [The venues of pre-1956 visits. Ed.]

While Mr. Smith took his group off to do some simple surveying, Mr. Liversidge's group enjoyed themselves making pastel pictures and Mr. Slade's were studying nature, Joe took a group to look at trees. 'Their most interesting find was an elm tree completely covered by small caterpillars which were wrapped in yards of silvery web – the whole thing like one of the more horrific Disney cartoons.' [An early sighting of Dutch Elm disease perhaps. Ed.]

'Sun-tanned and a little weary, we returned to our buses, some to read, a few to finish the quiz, and not a few to sleep. It had been a full programme and one of those lovely days for which we shall remember June 1959.'

1960 saw the introduction of yet another new 'story' told in the grounds of Pickering Castle, that of the visit of the barons in 1036 to farmer Morcar for the compilation of the Domesday Book and of Edward II's hunting party with Thomas, the Earl of Lancaster. Joe pointed out to the students that such tales lend themselves to imaginative written work and drawing when the children return to school.

On entering Pickering Church it was always normal practice for pupils and students to kneel in prayer for a few moments. In 1962 the vicar, on seeing this, remarked on the rarity of such behaviour 'in these days'.

Joe must have been a little conscious of the fact that the annual Primary trips were being made to the same places – he was always one for a change. In the notes he says, rather apologetically, – 'As the Pickering-Goathland route has proved the favourite we repeated that excursion. It was new to the children and students'.

This was to be Joe's last excursion with the Primary Department but not the last he was to help organise. Several Old Student's brought children to York from their far-flung places of work and Joe used to help them with the arrangements 'at this end'. He made notes of St. Mary's Abbey, the Minster and other places of interest and sent them off to be made into many more 'quiz booklets' by ex-Johnsmen.

The Open Day exhibits in the Porch Room continued to be as diverse and exiting as ever although no reports of them appear in *The White Rose's* of 1962 or 1963, the year Joe retired. However, he kept up the high standards he had set for himself right to the end, there was no 'slacking off' in his make up.

Joe was very careful not to interfere with the work of his successors in the numerous fields of his activities, although at times it must have been tempting to do so, but he was always very willing to assist them in any way he could – when asked. He must have noticed some dramatic changes, but then, Joe must have been a very hard act to follow. His willingness to work for the good of others, his vitality and his hard-won experience were not something that others possessed in the same measure. At the same time the College Joe had known over the past thirty-six years was changing rapidly and the new students had a much different outlook on life from that which he had been used to.

J.R.C's retirement in 1963 is the subject of the next section but as you will see he did not 'lie down' straight away but continued as a part-time Tutor-cum-Gardener at the Croft. Mr. Joseph Mountain, one time tutor in gardening but now in charge of all the College gardens, and Bernard his assistant would, no doubt, be shaken out of their normal, gentle routine with Joe's arrival!

Joe's organisational and theatrical skills were to be fully exploited at The Croft for a further five years. Later still he organised dances for the Old Johnsmen in the College dining hall, in the Merchant Taylor's Hall and at the Chase Hotel on Tadcaster Road which were all memorable events and amply lived up to the 'Copping Standard', providing many of his 'Matrimonial Agency' partners and other couples with some very enjoyable evening's entertainment.

CHAPTER VII

Mr. Copping Retires

THERE ARE FEW PEOPLE who become legends in their own lifetime but Joe was one of the 'few'. By the age of sixty he had taught children and students for a period of forty-three years, four in Worstead and thirty-nine in York. He was to continue for yet another five in a part-time capacity. No mean record.

In 1963 *The White Rose* magazine contained the following appreciations of his twenty-six years as a Tutor at St. John's. It is headed simply ....

JOE

JOSEPH ROBERT COPPING, known affectionately and universally as Joe, first came to St. John's as a student in 1921[*sic*]; he returned as a member of the Staff in 1937. This year he retires and below we print some extracts from recollections of him written by people who have known him as student, colleague and friend.

The Principal (Cannon P. J.Lamb) writes:

As you read on you will see that my more eloquent colleagues, whose appreciations I have read already, have excellently performed the pleasant and stimulating task of describing Mr. Copping. They have drawn him to the life. My part is to use this opportunity of expressing more formally the very deep sense of gratitude which the complex entity which we call St. John's College, York, feels towards a man who over a long period of years has served it supremely well. On behalf of the Governing Body, the staff, students past and present and all who have come under his benign and gay influence either at first hand or more remotely through those whom his work has inspired, I say to J.R.C. *Well done. Thank you.*

The Bursar, Mr. S. Watkin, writes:

.... Joe Copping is the only genius I know personally.

His many and varied gifts spring from an abundant vitality: from his early morning tea service to the end of his social engagements in the evening he brings zest and imagination to a myriad of tasks.

The tea service, not an unmitigated blessing for his less energetic colleagues, illustrates his kindness, practicality and love of company. It has been said, in the days before he retreated to another place, that the early morning brew was timed to serve equally well as a nightcap for a colleague of somewhat different daily routine ....

In twenty-five years Joe has slowed down physically at least enough to make the idea of taking a walk with him a feasible proposition. When only a little younger his legs, like his mind today, skipped and jumped and ran ahead of more pedestrian colleagues. But it is never wise to assume that his mind has lost its agility; he is seldom ignorant of the latest educational idea and usually recalls when it was last in vogue.... I do not think he would describe himself as a student of formal Psychology, but few will deny that he used psychology brilliantly both in and out of the classroom. For him teaching remains an art to be practiced, something that cannot be acquired from books but only by sensitive observation and experience in the school.... But it is not merely that he could teach anything; he could do most things. He is no mean musician, much more than an illustrator in water colours, has the greenest of fingers, plays bridge like Cuthbertson, writes reviews good enough to save I.T.V. from Pilkington and is something of a poet....

Whatever he may be as a musician or author there can be no doubt that when he followed his vocation to teaching, the professional stage lost a great producer, particularly in the field of comedy.... A teacher is perhaps best judged by the respect of his former pupils. Very many old students have told me that the thing they valued most dearly and have found most useful in their careers was the time spent with Joe Copping at College. They think of him not just as Joe the 'universal' teacher, but as 'The Master of our Revels' and as a personal friend.

It is beyond the power of institutions to honour their most distinguished members; the honour passes the other way. But there might be less to criticise in our educational system if it were flexible enough to recognise men like Joseph Robert Copping for what they are – Masters of Education.

He was also master of the 'last word' and I hope I shall be forgiven for recording his quip on a matter of religious knowledge teaching: 'Very well, in future, I shall tell the children that once upon a time there wasn't a man named Noah and he didn't have an ark'.

Mr. Duncan Edington, an Old Johnsman and a member of the teaching staff writes:

.... I first heard of Joe in my first year at College. He was famed for his portrayal of Olivia in *Twelfth Night*, – in a traditional production with the women's parts played by men. This seems ironic when we remember his brilliant productions of plays such as *The Tempest* where he employed such charming and capable actresses. Not only did he break this monastic tradition of only playing men in classical plays, but he also introduced more modern

Joe as Fagin in 'Pick-a-Pocket'.

and lighter plays such as *Who Killed the Count* and *Arsenic and Old Lace*. The Variety Shows were probably in his blood from the old 'Saturday Nights' in College. Under his direction they blossomed forth as lavish and polished productions. These were not only a source of pleasure to students and friends of the College, but they provided a vehicle by which Joe gave confidence to some of the more retiring students who thereby added sparkle to their teaching.

Another side of College life owes its inception to Joe. He joined the staff when Dr. Welch was blowing a 'breath of fresh air' through the old ways. Here Joe made a positive contribution by providing an outlet for some of the consequent freedom. He started the Saturday Night Dances and not only taught many students how to dance but also provided them with partners – often for life ....

Pictures of Joe crowd the mind; of him in his old dressing gown running across the lawn, of him sitting in his room in the midst of illustrations, cyclostyled sheets, boxes of everything one might need, of him encouraging the hesitant student and humbling the forward one, of him going to bed late and getting up early, of him hating to go to meetings and being restricted, of him planning the next holiday and the one after that....

What would he really like to have been? A Noel Coward, a Victor Sylvester, a travel agent, a village schoolmaster? No, I really think that all the time there has been a landscape gardener trying to get out!

Mr. Wakinshaw, this year's Senior Student, writes:

'Put the children first.' 'The children are more important than the subject.' These are the sentiments of Mr. Copping which countless Johnsmen have taken with them into the schools. Now, however, I realise that it is not only children that he regards as important but people in general.

This concern for people has ben exemplified for me by the way in which he has always taken such pains to get to know and understand his students. I shall always remember his readiness and willingness to advise, to guide, to stimulate and encourage his students.

Mr. Copping must know that with him in his retirement he takes the affection and high regard of the students whom he has taught.

Mr. J. Netherwood, an Old Johnsman (1930-32) and a former colleague, writes:

On leaving College I was appointed, with two other Johnsmen, to the staff of the Manor Higher Grade School, York. We met the head, a rather heavy and pompous individual, before going down. In August we returned to York and on Monday morning reported for our first day as probationary teachers.

Instead of the self-assured, well-built man we had seen at the interview, we were greeted by a slight, nervy and obviously harassed man, who had reached what seemed to us the mature age of 28. The head had been dispatched ignominiously and the acting head for our first term was Joe Copping. No one could have wished for a wiser or more considerate mentor at the start of a teaching career.

For the next six years, under two headmasters, Joe was the inspiration that turned a staff of twelve young men into as keen a team as could be found in any school anywhere. His complete devotion to the welfare of all boys in the school was infectious.

More than a thousand of York's middle-aged men have good cause to remember Joe as one of the highlights of their time in school. I must have met hundreds of Old Manor Boys, either as parents of my scholars or incidentally about the city and all ask about him as the one man they can easily remember. There is hesitation over the names of other members of the staff; Joe's personality left an indelible mark on all who came in contact with him.

His resourcefulness, inspiration and industry as a teacher were wonderful spurs to the rest of the staff.... I have only one small quarrel with him. As we were both called Joe, J.R.C. used to refer to me a Jeroboam and to himself as Rehoboam. I forgive him the implications which might arise from a study of the lives of these two reprobates but I really would have to change I Kings 14.v.30 substituting 'deep affection' for 'war'.

My one wish for Joseph R. Copping is that the next 31 years will be as rewarding to our mutual friendship as the past 31 have been....

The Vice-Principal, Mr. W. C. Chapman, writes:

It is impossible to think of College without the lively presence of Joe, just as it is incredible to think of him as in any sense ready for retirement. Like hundreds of students who have come in contact with him I have always found his spirit infectious; where he has touched the education of the students there one finds humour, vitality and a zest for experience. So many have found in him one who has patience and insight into their problems....

I can think of a host of things I remember about him; marking lessons at 6.30 a.m., teaching Lady Astor to do the Lambeth Walk, organising variety shows, climbing Bowfell, drinking rum and on one occasion substituting the usual Grace before tea, 'Sit down; It's kippers!'

In all his life with us here he has set us the good example in teaching education by his concern with children and to see Joe in a classroom or at Goathland or organising a Christmas Carol Service was to see someone living out the College motto and bringing out the abundance of life which is at the heart of all true education.

I can never express in mere words what his friendship has meant to me, but through it I have come to know more fully the meaning of the words loyalty and devotion. I can only hope that in his retirement he will find the happiness which he has brought in such full measure to others.

FLOREAT JOE

In the *SPREAD EAGLE* of 1964 – the magazine of the Old Students Association – was printed:

AN APPRECIATION BY JOE NETHERWOOD

I can think of many people who are far more competent than I am to write about Joe Copping. The only reason I agreed to it was that by the time the Editor asked me it was too near the printer's dead-line to approach anyone else and I have been a friend of his for 32 years.

Joe is a decidedly odd chap. He is the only man I know who has become younger as he has aged. At 28 he was (in school at any rate) a middle-aged man; at 60 he is completely 'with it'. If he were not such a fastidious person I should expect to see him with a Beatle cut and the clothes to match.

He must be the best known Old Johnsman alive. In York itself he has a considerable number of friends who remember him chiefly for his production of the stage shows of the Young Teachers. He wrote, produced, stage-managed and generally inspired, topical reviews and pantomimes from 1932 to 1939. Hundreds of Old Manor Boys remember him with affection and gratitude for the way in which he could inspire a respect for learning and a feeling that each boy mattered. To help pay for a new floor for the gym, he organised Whist and Bridge Drives with the air of a professional M.C. but was as exuberant as a young schoolboy when we were in camp. He was the leading-light in the occasional end-of-term booze-up, but the following morning could march down the aisle to play the organ, looking down his nose at the assembled boys and sorry-looking staff. At least three headmasters gained reputations based largely on J.R.C.

When he joined the staff of the College in 1937 it made a tremendous impact on the teachers of York. St. John's was taking on the strength someone who had taught for more than a dozen years in the type of school for which the men were trained. It was soon apparent that he was making his presence felt in College.

Over the years he has built up an Education Department with special regard for Primary Schools. In what might be considered his spare time he has organised Saturday evening dances which could be called York's Premier Matrimonial Academy. From the evidence of Johnsmen over the past 18 years I have not been able to discover which of these two functions is the more important.

The York Branch owes much to Joe Copping. About 15 years ago he came to see me during S.P. and said that he wanted to do something for the branch. He wondered what I thought about having a dance in College when the men had gone down in June. I was sure that we would welcome such a function. Joe made all the arrangements – we danced in the J.C.R. sat out to drink in the Inner Quad and enjoyed ourselves thoroughly. This private party and the Merchant Taylors' Hall dances which he M.C's are the biggest factors in holding us together.

He has 'arrangements' with landlords, gardens for old ladies, takes parties to entertain old people in homes, remembers anniversaries, names of wives and children of old students and calls the Vice-Principal unprintable names. We have something to look forward to when he is our President.

CHAPTER VIII

Joe at the Croft

JOE MOVED OUT OF his rooms in Lower New at Lord Mayor's Walk and took up residence in The Croft, ostensibly to help the gardeners and give some lectures on a part-time basis. In reality it was the College's way of easing him gently into full-time retirement. As we have come to know of Joe he was not one to take half measures and soon the 'Croft Socials' were to become imbued with his theatrical skills.

The 1963 programme shows twelve 'turns' which, in Joe's inimitable way, consisted of songs, mime and sketches both amusing and satirical – in essence a true 'variety'.

The Croft Hostel report in the magazine reads .... 'Owing to the splendid work of Mr. Copping who is a great asset to the Hostel, we have held three excellent Sunday Social evenings to which various members of the staff were invited and during which men of the Hostel displayed to the full their versatility as entertainers'. The old 'master' had not lost his touch!

In 1964 a similar format was followed – Joe's impeccably handwritten Programmes laid out 'sideways' on an A4 sheet and folded to A5 were, of course, cyclostyled. The 'Geordies' in song, 'Infidelity' (according to Shakespeare), Piano Duets, 'Infidelity' (according to Dylan Thomas), 'As in a Mirror' [He'd found another set of Twins! Ed.], 'Interview for an Education Tutor' and 'The Croft Singers' were on offer. Another, later 'famous' group had its debut at this show. Item 7 is headed 'Songs with Guitar' with two students who, soon to be joined by others became 'The Crofters' Band and carried on, well after they had all left College, playing at gigs and concerts around the county.

Hostel notes record: 'Once again we have enjoyed a most successful year at the Croft and a fine spirit has been much in evidence. Just before Christmas Mr. Copping produced another friendly and successful Croft Social Evening at which the talents of some of our members were ably displayed. Mr. Copping's artistic ability has proved a great asset to the Croft in other ways and one need only see the Hostel garden to realise that his "green fingers" have been at work'.

The next year, on November 28th, 1965 saw one of the last shows Joe produced. In *The White Rose* 1966 the President of the Croft Hostel writes: ....'As usual Mr. Copping put a great deal of energy into the "Croft Social", brightening up one of the many dull winter evenings of our first term; we thank him most sincerely and fully appreciate his help in all activities which have made this year such a successful one in the history of the Croft'.

Joe lived for five years at the Croft, working alongside 'Bill' Richardson, the Warden of the Hostel and between them they ran a very happy 'ship'. They often went on holiday together and with other members of the staff during College breaks. Whilst there, Joe helped the gardeners to take hundreds of geranium cuttings and plant thousands of bedding-plant seeds; he 'took over' the front garden and in Spring and Autumn it was a blaze of subtly combined areas of colour. He continued to give a few lectures and often demonstrated to students his amazing skill at blackboard work, His other 'love', of actively creating and organising a pleasant social life for the students was greatly appreciated by those living at the Croft and Joe had been happy to provide it.

A Chapel in Norfolk

It was while Joe was still living at The Croft in 1966 that he was persuaded by Chris Chapman to tell the story of his childhood to the students. Joe was very reluctant to talk about himself, but eventually he wove a 'religious' story around his upbringing in a Primitive Methodist family and his father's quest for a Chapel in the village.

The source of the tale that follows was gleaned from a very poor quality reel-to-reel tape recording together with some notes Joe had written down as an *aide memoire*. At times the student's laughter drowned out the words and I have had to put in question marks at these places. About 50 students, members of the S.C.M., were present at the talk.

'This is not a Religious Knowledge lecture as you may gather by the way everyone is sitting around tables – like a Blackpool .... (?) [Laughter] – I must say it's a great improvement on the days when everyone was sitting in serried rows.

This is a story of my childhood – and the 30 years before – which is as clear to me as if it were yesterday. Every word is true – that is why I am happy to have it recorded. It is a first-hand treatise of Nonconformity at its most rampant – I was brought up as a Primitive Methodist – the pariahs of the Protestant Church.

There are many rungs on the Christian ladder – There are the Roman Catholics – Henry XIII broke away from Rome and the Church of England was formed – they are known as Protestants. From the Church of England another break-away group was formed and the Nonconformists came into being. They again split into the Congregationalists, the Baptists, the Wesleyan Methodists – who didn't sing Psalms and wouldn't have any decorations in their chapels – and then there were the Primitive Methodists.

My father and mother were Primitive Methodists – no chance of Christian unity in those days – My father had two enemies – The Pope and the Devil. We have come a long way towards Christian Unity since then.

The Chapel was barn shaped – had no decorations whatsoever – there was a rostrum at one end with steps up at both sides – and a Mercy Seat – that was all.

My story cannot help but be amusing – but the people in it were Christians – followers of Christ – and attending a place of worship was the "fashion of their time". All the people I met had a simple faith – (?) like Salvation Army (?)

I was born in a Village called Worstead in north-east Norfolk – Half way between Norwich and Cromer – near North Walsham. It found fame in the 13th & 14th C. when 200 Flemish weavers were brought over to England by Edward III – The woollen trade was first in importance and Norfolk was the most prosperous county in England because of the cloth weaving. The village gave its name to Worsted Cloth, which was a very finely woven cloth – exported to Venice and Constantinople. Worstead was the third largest town in Norfolk after Norwich and Dunwich. It was a town of 4,000 people – the Black Death in the 1340's took two-thirds of the population – the Industrial Revolution took away many more. It is now a farming community of about 700 people.

My family is remarkable in only one respect – my grandfather was born 177 years ago at the time of the French Revolution in 1789. My father was born when grandfather was 57-years-old – the 23rd child – in 1845. I was born in 1903 when my father was 57-years-old.

In 1883 father moved from Hardwick (where my grandfather was a miller) to Worstead where he bought a Grocery-cum-Drapery store housed in an enormous rambling 14C building. It had low windows running from wall to wall – it had been used by the weavers who needed as much light as possible. There were many out-buildings and a large garden at the rear.

Father was a Primitive Methodist and although there was a Church in the village there was no Chapel. He would never go into a C. of E. Church – he was determined that at all costs there must be a Chapel in the village.

There were three prominent people who lived in the village. "Squire" Rous, Mrs. Russel-Day – who went round in a Bath Chair – and the Vicar named Breffitt – straight out of the Victorian era. They didn't want a Chapel and wouldn't sell any of their land so father chopped off a piece of his own garden and built it there. The cost of this Chapel was £300 and this was raised by my father and his Primitive Methodist friends. He set up a band known as Copping's Brass Band – Mr. Amis, a local farmer, lent his barn for concerts – they got uniforms and they travelled all around the area raising money (1882-1886). After four years "Copping's Chapel" was built in 1887. It was shaped like a barn with a door at one end, a rostrum with three steps up at each side of it and pews each side of Chapel. It had Hurricane Lamps hanging from the ceiling which pulled down to be cleaned and lit by the lady who cleaned the Chapel, with a piece of coconut matting on floor. (?) ....lane about a yard-wide at side of Chapel to get to the W.C. – It whiffed! [Laughter] There was a picture in the loo entitled "The Broad and Narrow Way". It showed hundreds of people on the broad path leading to the devil with only 2 or 3 on the narrow path. One of these was being attacked by a lion, but this way lead to Heaven. It hung over the loo but father moved it to a nail on the back of door so the ladies could see it. [Laughter]

In 1903 I was born and named Joseph (an addition). I was rather a surprise arrival!

There was a thriving business – grocery, drapery, general store and Post Office. Mother and father worked long hours. At 4.30 a.m. my step-sister Flo and I met the Mail Coach at the end of lane – Jimmy Slop was the driver's name. Shop opened 8.0 a.m. – closed 8.0 p.m. and at 10 p.m. on Saturdays. Cigarettes were 20 for 6d – [here Joe mentions other money differences]. Flo and I sorted letters ready for delivery. We NEVER worked on Sundays – nothing done – washing-up left until Monday morning – went to Chapel three times – Morning, Afternoon & Evening – Sundays was a thing apart, 4th C. "Heaven and Hell" were very real. My Mother was an indefatigable lady – she never had a holiday.

The Chapel was part of North Walsham Circuit – Nth. Walsham famous for its Grammar School where Nelson attended. It had one Minister and 80 Local Preachers – people who felt the urge to preach. They walked, cycled or came in pony trap to our Chapel – sometimes brought their wife and family – mother always provided tea for them. Amazing people – Uneducated but not Unintelligent – they had had no opportunities for education but often gave quite brilliant sermons. To become a local preacher you needed a Birth Certificate and had to preach one sermon in front of three other preachers.

George Bloom – children loved him – he talked through his nose – Story of Good Samaritan – the one who passed by on the other side was a "Rascal". When I was in my 2nd Yr at College – went home and he told story of Jonah & the Whale ....(?) [Laughter]

Modicar Bircham – had three sons – Adam, Jonah & Bordica? – he couldn't read too well and when he came to a long or difficult word in the Bible used to say "hard word" and carry on reading. "And Saul came to the city of '*hard word*' and said unto the people...." John Hill – was in the middle of telling a story .... "Jesus said, Watch and Pray".... when the door burst open and a woman shouted in, "Can I borrow your (bicycle) Pump?" Often the services were very informal goings-on. Dick Gibson – child in service making a noise – Dick had a loud voice and he said "Let it cry madam – I can shout over it!"

When I was ten-years-old I started playing the harmonium, which had "stoppers" (organ stops). One of these came right out if pulled too hard. It was foot pumped – [here Joe sat at a desk and gave a demonstration of how it was done] – I had to get pumping just before the end of the Bible reading – I got used to it in time so that the music started up without a long, "pregnant" pause.

Sankeys – like folk songs – (similar to negro or pop songs today) [Ira D. Sankey wrote 200-300 of these songs in conjunction with a man named Moody who wrote the music.] We always sat down to sing these. Afternoon service – 1 hymn and a Sankey: Evening 3 hymns and a Sankey. They had an easy chorus which those who couldn't read could soon pick up. [Here Joe sang some of the Sankeys –]

Harvest Festival – "Bringing in the Sheaves – bringing in the sheaves
We shall come rejoicing – bringing in the sheaves".

And another .... "When the roll is called up yonder .... I'll be there".

There was no monotony – always some Highlights throughout year – often to raise money for the Chapel.

Camp Meeting: Once a year 3 preachers came – paraded round village on a wagonette singing Sankeys – at 2.30 everyone joined in procession and went to ammunition meadow. Field with enormous "hollow" 15ft deep – it was said to be where 2,700 people were buried after Black Death in 1346 – bodies decomposed and earth fallen in.

Tea Meetings 6d: Service of Songs at Whitsuntide using books like "Rhoda" – The Gipsy Girls' Mission of Love. Readings interspersed with songs. On the 1st (?) .... in every Quarter – held Supper meetings.

Christmas – People put their names on piece of paper with amount of giving on the Trees – there were Gold & Silver Trees.... (?) The papers then taken off one by one and read out – "God Loveth – Mrs. Lyres 2/6" – "Give thine alms to God in secret – Anon 10/6".

Harvest Festivals: Auction after Service of all produce that had been given – Harry Broom the butcher was Auctioneer – Flo jotted down amounts raised and names of the buyers. People sat in Chapel chewing apples and cracking nuts as soon as they had bought them – [Laughter]. Niece Muriel had high falsetto voice, she would insist on singing a solo, which was awful – [Here Joe gave a "sample" of Muriel's voice] – I told her "I warned you so!" [More laughter]

I went to Worstead (C of E) School. In 1917 Mrs. Colthorpe my teacher, at the end of an arithmetic lesson said "Anyone want to be a Teacher?" – that's when "The rot set in" for me!

Whatever might be thought of these people – they were Christians – with a simple faith.'

Postscript: I've been back to Worstead since – Norwich House now made into flats. Village main industry – Packing Bird's Eye Peas. No Vicar – one now covers 4 parishes – (Seat on loo ??). Chapel – had a 'proper' organ, Hymn Boards, Electric lights, – No Sankeys. Eight years ago, closed as a Chapel and now used by St. John's Ambulance Brigade.

CHAPTER IX

Retirement – Full-Time

IN THE JULY OF 1968, after living for five years at The Croft and, as it were, 'winding down' just a little after forty–three years of full-time teaching and lecturing, Joe took up residence in one of Mrs. Towler's flats in Bootham Terrace, the ground floor of number thirteen.

He had previously leased another of Mrs. T's flats – the Top Floor, No. 1 Bootham Terrace – while still resident in the Main College. This comprised two or three rooms built in the roof space of the four-storey terrace house, quite small but, made so by Joe, very cosy and welcoming. He used this as a 'retreat' when he felt like escaping from the College confines and whenever he wished to entertain or 'put-up' visiting guests.

The new flat was much larger, as Joe rented the whole of the ground floor and had 'charge' of the long back garden. He soon put his own 'stamp' on it, decorating it tastefully and moving his personal furniture in. A brief note in his diary says, – Hunters N.B.G. – went to Leaks instead for curtains! Joe wasn't one for writing long entries in his A4 size 'Boots' Scribbling Dairies, those for the years 1968 to 1978 being extant, but such notes as there are provide a vivid picture of the hectic life he led during this period.

For many years he had gone up to London during the Christmas break, stayed with old students or other friends and taken in some of the latest shows. In December 1967 he saw *Half-a-Sixpence* and *Dr. Zhivago* and was going to Drury Lane but was prevented from doing so because he had a bout of Bronchitis and had to return to The Croft where, he writes, 'it was lovely and warm'. These London trips continued and were often combined with a visit to the Southern Branch of the Old Student's Association, of which Harold Hogarth a good friend and oft-times host to Joe, was a leading member. In January 1969 he mentions seeing *Oh Clarence* with the O.J.; 1970 The Royal Ballet; 1971 *Sleuth* and *Viola Regina*; 1972 a visit to Drury Lane and in 1974 *Dandy Dick* at the Garrick as well as the Pantomime at the Palladium.

During the first part of the Summer holidays Joe usually visited his home county taking in Ipswich, Norwich, Worstead, Hethersett and Cromer, at all of which places he had friends or relations. Then, he normally took a fortnight's holiday abroad – Ibiza, Majorca, Seefeld, Austria, Tremezzo, Innsbruck, Madeira and Malta being some of the foreign places he visited during his retirement. He also liked to visit Scotland and the Lake District whenever he took an 'extra' holiday.

As has already been mentioned these holidays were planned very carefully beforehand, a full written diary was kept during them and afterwards the photographs (normally slides) were selected into 'showable' collections. He always wrote interesting notes and comments about each slide and rehearsed his presentations at home before showing them. Because of this careful preparation Joe managed to show other people his 'holiday snaps' without them becoming bored stiff half way through – as normally happens. His knack of making the narrative interesting and strictly limiting the number of slides made such shows a delight to watch.

Some of his holiday diaries survive. They contain pressed flowers, sketch maps, thumb-nail drawings (which he would later use for his larger paintings) and souvenir postcards of places visited. Many times he assisted people, who were going to a place he had recently visited, by giving them first-hand knowledge of the area.

J.R.C. had always been quite a keen photographer and in retirement he combined this hobby with painting. He attended day and evening classes (Painting for Pleasure) for both watercolour and oil painting and became very proficient using either medium. Most of his pictures went to his few remaining relatives when he died but one or two, including drafts and pastel drawing still remain in York. His artistic works ranged from self portraits, and portraits through to still-lifes and landscapes but he seldom displayed them in his own flat. At a later date, when Joe went into a Nursing Home, I hung some of them in his bedroom there.

Not content with painting classes, Joe decided he would also attend 'Party Cookery' classes and this he did for several sessions, under the watchful eye of Mrs. Jean Woods. He enjoyed cooking, both for himself and for the many dinner and supper parties he gave. Sometimes he would try out a new recipe he had just learned on us before offering it to some special guests who were shortly to be entertained.

As was typical of Joe his retirement days were filled almost as full as his working days had been. He was able to do more 'visiting' than before and usually walked into the city centre each morning for 'a cup of tea and a cake at Bettys'. As well as looking after the garden at number 13, he kept Mrs. Towler's garden tidy, still helped with the front garden at The Croft and, when 'Lenny' Poore retired from College to live at Great Edstone, totally re-organised the garden there and planted it up for him.

One very poignant set of entries in Joe's diary for 1973 read:

May 21: To Croft – Wattys (for coffee) [Mr. Stanley Watkins.]
May 22: Watty dead. Bill [Richardson] found him last night (heart attack)
May 23: Wattys gardening [This crossed out Ed.]
May 25: Funeral Meet at Chris' 12.30 [Chris Chapman.]

Mr. Watkin had retired as the Bursar at College the previous year and had made his home in a house situated on the corner of Deangate and The Queens Path near the Minster. Joe was in the process of re-organising and planting-up the garden.

As one gets older death becomes a closer companion and many entries in the diaries record the passing of Joe's good friends, some relations, quite a few ex-colleagues and some others with whom he had played cards or dominoes on a regular basis. But he was a pragmatic fellow and, although these losses must have been deeply felt, he got on with his own life.

Some of the less sombre entries in the diaries – curt and to the point as they always were – may raise a smile or two:

May 3 1969	– get Italian up to date	
May 12	– Gave up smoking – again. Jess avers to gum	
July 18	– GAVE UP SMOKING	
Nov 21	– Gave up smoking again – gave Fred SIX	
Dec 16	– Marygate whoopee	
Dec 31	– sore throat – gave up smoking	
Jan 1 1970	– gave up smoking	
Apr 19	– did Jessies garden	[Jessie Ellis]

Sept 19	–	To Dent with Judy & David if fine. Gave up smoking
Sept 12	–	Nijinsky wins St. Leger 2/7
Dec 19	–	shopping lunacy
Jan 17 1971	–	painted picture. Abbey at Sunset
Feb 21	–	Song for Europe – 1) Look Left Look Right – verse not so good as (3). 2) In My World – rather ordinary rhythm. 3) Jack in the Box – Puppet – but not so la la. 4) Another Time – little appeal. 5) Wind of Change – too quick. 6) Someone to Love Me – Charming, clear but no Lulu vim or Sandie mystery. Rhythm mechanical. [Joe ringed 1 and 3 as being his choices. Ed.]
May 20	–	Ma..s and S..n for meal – no spices in the food!
Nov 13	–	gave up smoking
Nov 25	–	11 days – no cigs
Jan 16 1972	–	Sleep – over sherried
May 7 1973	–	(70)
May 11	–	Wonderful party at Stonewold – [See 'This is your Life' party below. Ed]
Aug 24	–	Invasion from Brompton
Jan 2 1974	–	Gave up smoking again
Apr 6	–	Gave up smoking
Nov 7	–	Bettys alone – What a lunch – Never again – soup, plaice, parsley sauce, chips, peas. Fruit, cream
Dec 28	–	Golly woobles
Dec 29	–	still up in night
Feb 12 1975	–	Lent – gave up smoking
Feb 23	–	Gave up smoking
March 19	–	Post – gone up to 7p!!!
May 5	–	Gardening 'till dropped' ....

Although it may seem amusing to read that Joe was always 'giving up smoking', part of the reason was that, prior to holidays, he saved the money not spent on his favourite 'Craven A' cigarettes in a jar and then used this for his 'spending money' when abroad.

Mention is made in the foregoing entries of Joe's 70th Birthday Party at Stonewold. John and Audrey James, my wife and I decided to 'fix' a 'This is Your Life' stunt for this occasion. Audrey asked

Chris Chapman (who acted the 'Eammon Andrews' part) and Joe for a meal – which she often did – and everyone else arrived early and hid in the back room. Then Chris began to read Joe's 'Life' and the rest of us appeared one at a time and 'said our piece'. Principal Philip Lamb and his wife Helen were there as well as Leonard Poore, Stanley Watkin, Jim and Marion Shields, Fred and Gwen Pickard (who helped Joe considerably after the Air-Raid tragedy), Jean Buckle (who often took a part in the College Plays), Jessie Ellis – a card playing partner, Mrs. Woods his cookery tutor and Tony Cleaver. 'The Book' still exists, complete with photographs and the signatures of all who were there, and will eventually find its way – along with his other papers – into the Copping 'archives' at College.

Joe's diaries show that he was an active supporter of the Old Students Association (Old Johnsmen) at both National and Branch level. Many entries show his involvement by attending meetings, joining in with the activities organised by Branch members sometimes as an invited guest – and by helping to organise dances and dinners for Old Students, especially of the York Branch.

In 1964, just after he had 'retired' from full-time work but was living at The Croft, he was elected Vice-President of the National O.S.A. The following year he took up the Presidency and wrote the following message in *The Spread Eagle* – 1965:

THE PRESIDENT WRITES

The Croft Hostel
(St. John's College)
19 Heworth Green
York

GREETINGS –

– To all Old Johnsmen who still have an interest in their College and receive a copy of 'Spread Eagle' No. 8.

– To the faithful 'ancients' who for more than forty years have remembered the friends they made in the 'hutches' round the quad. I used to wonder why so many old men came to reunion. Now I know.

– To the young men and women who are leaving college this year. Become life members of this Association. I shall always remember the first young ladies to complete their three-year course, 'the magnificent seven', and I hope to see one of you become our first Woman President.

– To the thousands of students I knew so well in the years 1937 to 1963, especially those of the war and post-war years, who in adverse conditions, had to provide their own recreation. We shall never forget those 'black-out' dances, the crowded Music Circles and the fun we had on the old Lecture Theatre stage. 'Sweet are the uses of adversity' was never more true than in those dark days before the Welfare State, when Bede, Saltley and Cheltenham joined us for a time. Two of my greatest friends are Bede-Johnsmen.

– To the hundred plus who found a 'mate' at the Saturday Evening 'Marriage Market'.

– To the 'four corners of the earth' where Old Johnsmen are not forgotten. They are working in the 'Vineyards' of all the Continents except Antarctica. Recently I heard from Robin Wardell (Rural Science 1961-63) who is 'plying his trade' as Agricultural Officer on the Gilbert and Ellis Island Colony in the West Pacific. The atlas tells me that it is impossible to get farther from York until we have a Johnsman on the moon.

– To all past Presidents including Ex-President Albert Hall and to Mr. Pickering who takes over from me on July 3rd.

– To Tony Slack the Editor of this magazine. I feel ashamed that in spite of his appeal for Year secretaries, my own year ('22-'24) remains un-represented. I know I've retired but so have the rest.

– And lastly my greetings to that exclusive group of men called Secretaries, to all who collect information from men of their year and provide the Newsletter Service, to the Secretaries of the Branches and to Mr. J. T. Firth our General Secretary. It is a pleasant honour to be a President and wear the ribboned medal, but as we all know our Association thrives on the work of a few secretaries whose names are in 'Spread Eagle'. To them we say 'thank you'.

JOE COPPING

J.R.C. was also a member of the local York Branch and was it's President either two or three times over the years. In February '69 he was instrumental in organising an O.J. party at the Croft, Dinner Dances at the Chase Hotel in the November of '70 and again in

’72 with yet another in March 1975. He always acted as M.C. and made sure that everyone took their full part in the dancing. If there were any ‘unattached’ ladies, Joe always saw to it that they got plenty of dances during the evening, either with himself or with other ‘spare’ males. In his day ‘couples’, whether married or not, seldom danced with each other for the whole evening – everyone was encouraged to dance with a different partner for at least some of the dances. Only when it came to The Last Waltz, invariably ‘Lebenstraum’, did all couples get back together again.

For Joe, life in retirement was a social whirl of visiting, being visited – many times by old Johnsmen, their wives and families – and holidays – both abroad and in Britain. He kept in touch with the College, his former colleagues, many of whom had by this time themselves retired, and with the many events which took place locally.

All went well until about 1979 when close friends realised that, although he was still physically fit and agile, he was beginning to lose his memory and was not feeding himself properly. Theo Ross, a retired teacher whom Joe had known from many years before, was very kind – took him out for meals and trips in her car and generally ‘mothered’ him. Other close friends, equally as generous and concerned, invited him for meals and generally kept a ‘watching brief’ over him.

Soon it became obvious that he would need to be looked after around-the-clock so, in late 1980, Joe took up residence in a private Nursing Home at ‘Burton Croft’ in Burton Stone Lane.

The last five years of Joe’s life are not something I wish to write about, but sufficient for it to be said that during all of them he was well looked after, and was not forgotten.

Joseph Robert Copping died peacefully in his sleep during the night of 27/28th September 1985 a few hours after we had said the Lord’s Prayer together and I had bid him ‘Good Night’.

A Selfless man who, for Others, Lived his Life ....
.... UT VITAM HABEANT ET ABUNDANTIUS

[.... That they may have Life and have it more abundantly.
St. John Ch.10 verse x]

Epilogue

IT IS SAID THAT some are born to teach while others are born teachers.

During his time under training for and as a teacher, Joe Copping worked under four Headmasters and four Principles. All of them, and here I am presuming that Headmaster Ford eventually gave Joe a good reference in order to gain a College place, spoke in glowing terms of his expertise as a born teacher. Mr. Cooper, Headmaster of the Manor School, went as far as to say that he was 'the greatest teacher (he) had ever met'. Mr. Watkin described him as 'a genius'.

None of the accolades heaped upon him were exaggerations – they were, in a way, the best means people could find to express their admiration of a man whom it was almost impossible to describe in mere words. The sheer magnitude of his personality, of his abilities as a 'teacher' and of his total immersion in and commitment to everything he undertook are indescribable. Yet, he was such a modest, unassuming man.

On more than one occasion during his life Joe applied for Headmasterships but for reasons, now known only to himself, these never materialised. If they had, many children would have gained that which many students gained instead and hopefully they, in turn, passed on to many, many more children. In a way his 'teachings' spread far wider than ever they could have, had he been based in just one school.

Joe seldom talked about himself nor did he ever have a wrong word to say about anyone else and he never 'grumbled'. However, like his father before him, Joe too had an 'enemy', his was not the Pope but CHEESE! He couldn't stand the stuff.

He was always willing to listen to other people, to their worries or their problems and he was the first to help those in need of reassurance or encouragement. I have yet to meet or hear about anyone who did not ‘like’ Joe. The many reminiscences, penned by Old Johnsmen and printed in the College magazines, invariably mention Joe in one way or another. He was the kind of man you never forgot.

He held deep Christian beliefs, even though at times he was rather flippant, but never irreverent, about Church of England Services. On one occasion, after the responses ‘Lord, have mercy upon us. Christ have mercy upon us. Lord have mercy upon us’. Joe was heard to mutter – ‘He would have heard us the first time!’ This matter-of-factness was one of his endearing characteristics which brought many a smile to other’s lips. That classic ‘grace’ uttered, without a glimmer of a smile, from the top table in the dining room – ‘Sit down. It’s kippers’ – could only have been said by Joe.

His native upbringing in Norfolk within a Primitive Methodist family background gave him a ‘no frills’ approach to life which, without being irreligious or boorish, gave him a certain droll propensity unique to himself. At times, if he wished to extricate himself from some difficult situation or some discussion he did not want to pursue, he would ‘act gormless’ and pretend he didn’t know or hadn’t heard. At others, especially at meetings, many of which he considered a ‘waste of time’, if he thought the discussion had gone on long enough he would come out with some ‘to the point – practical suggestion’ which usually brought matters quickly to a head. He was a master of the ‘last word’.

There will be many little snippets of Joe’s wry sense of humour that are stored in so many peoples’ memories that they alone could make a sizeable treatise; but Joe was not a man to look back, he was a man of today and tomorrow, a man who did not forget but at the same time used past experiences to shape what he did and was.

In a book of this nature, looking back is all one can reasonably do, but at this stage we too can now look forward and be proud to know that Joe Copping’s name is still prominently displayed in the Lord Mayor’s Walk premises of the University College of Ripon and York, St. John.

This has come about mainly through the good offices and patient persistence of John Maw, a student and tutor of the College, following T. Cluderay’s suggestion that a memorial fund be set up. The idea of a Primary Education room, equipped with up-to-date resources, which the current students could use, was decided upon. Joe's 'own' Porch room unfortunately could not be used, so instead the room to the left of the bell-tower archway was officially named 'The Copping Room' on 14th March 1992. Chris Chapman dedicated the room with the following words – embellished, of course, in his own unique manner:

> 'I am glad to see the name of Joe Copping embedded in the architectural layout of the College. Old students of the pre-1963 era will rejoice with me over this memorable man. Why memorable? He was quite one of the funniest characters I have ever encountered. He was a country boy in Norfolk, a child of old parents, serving in the village emporium in the days of the pony and trap and playing the harmonium in the Methodist Chapel, built in the Copping's back garden.... He smoked 35 Craven 'A' a day – and gave Health Education lectures! He loved life. He was a warm, witty and human man. He brought hope to many a despairing novice teacher and he brought convivial joy to the Senior Common Room. So in the hearts of his friends, among them very many old students, he is not to die. Today we still salute Dear Joe.'

A total amount of £2,786 was raised by former students for the fund, which was handed over to the College to help equip the room.

In 1995, because of the ever constant reorganisations within the College buildings, the Primary Education Department had to be re-located, the Joe Copping Room is now situated in the co-joined front bedrooms of what, until recently, was the Principal's House. Joe would smile at that!

His framed portrait together with a similarly framed short biography hang above the fireplace and I hope that a copy of this work and some of his 'treasures', that I have drawn upon to quote in it, will shortly take their place in 'his room' too.

As I reach the last paragraph I am very conscious that this book tends to eulogise Joe, perhaps beyond belief. I can make no apology for this, because every word that is written in it is true.

Whether it is possible or not for someone who did not meet Joe Copping to comprehend that such a man once lived and breathed, once was such a unique 'teacher' among teachers, once was and did all the things outlined within these pages and a great deal more that are not – I can only say ....

THIS WAS HIS LIFE.

Appendices

[A] An Appreciation – The Rev. Professor A. A. Cock
[B] Mum's Last Letter
[C] Travels with Joe Copping

PRINCIPAL THE REV. PROFESSOR Albert A. Cock left St. John's in 1945. He wrote this appreciation of Joe at the time. I append it for historical reasons as it does not appear in the main body of the text:

ST JOHN'S COLLEGE, YORK
Telephone 3596
THE PRINCIPAL The Rev. Professor A. A. COCK
2nd July 1954

It is with exceptional pleasure that I place on record my appreciation of the services rendered to this College during many years, and particularly during the six years of my own tenure of office as principal, of Mr. Joseph Copping. They have been war years and the College, like other institutions, has had its own share of sufferings and Mr. Copping, too, had his own private and grievous suffering. Nevertheless, his remarkable skill in teaching, his versatility, his great creative power of friendship have endeared him to many generations of students and staff alike, and is rightly known as Joseph, the well-beloved.

Mr. Copping has done extremely good work in our school practice and in practical teaching method. He has been of extraordinary service in his teaching of Geography. He has given our men first-rate instruction in Hygiene. He has taken the Ordinary Music Course with great distinction and success. He has controlled our Chapel Choir, both for ordinary and extraordinary occasions with brilliance and beauty. He has shown a superb flair for organising and conducting our social life, particularly at weekends. He has organised student dances of a quite unusually high character, musical evenings on Saturdays and Sundays which are a distinct feature of the life of this College during the past six years and he has produced many a play and brought out the latent talent of many a student for dramatics.

He is greatly beloved in all our schools and amongst all my colleagues. He has earned the life-long devotion of many a student because of the beauty and simplicity of his character. He has a very great sense of humour and keeps the High Table healthy by his knowledge of dietetics. There must be exceedingly few colleges that possess so richly gifted a man as Mr. Copping and none that possesses a more devout Christian. He is an excellent preacher.

(Signed) Albert A. Cock
Principal, St. John's College, York
Fellow of King's College, London
Formerly Vice-Principal and Professor of Education
and Philosophy, University College, Southampton

Joe's mother – that indefatigable lady – died, aged 81, shortly after this letter was sent to his marital home in 1938. The envelope, on which Joe has written in pencil, 'mum's last letter', unfortunately contains only one page of the letter, written on both sides. I have included it here for two reasons; Joe must have thought a great deal of it – he was not normally a 'saver of things' – and because it is a piece of social history.

Addressed to: Mr. J. R. Copping, 3 Fairway, Rawcliffe Lane, York.

Norwich House
Worstead
Oct 6/38
Thur eve

My Dear Joe,

Thanks for your letter. Yes I have been looking for a letter to know how you were getting on during those anxious days last week thank God through His providence & the prayers of His people that we are brought through a great Crisis which we might now have been involved in. Its wonderful how Mr. Chamberlain went through it & what a welcome(d) he had on his return on Friday & now some of the opposition party w(h)ant to pick him to pieces seem like it.

Last Thursday the gas masks were given out at the Mens Club Room, the Drurys came & fitted me Friday morning as I did not feel well enough to go there. I hope we may never want them, have you and Marjorie been fitted, they are not quite so bad as we've seen them in the papers.

Did you hear the Archbishop of Canterbury on the wireless last Sunday (week) [crossed out. Ed.] & during the week and how calm & good he was. Ben is wonderfully strung up on the war news talking to every traveller that comes into the shop, they have gone to Nth Walsham this afternoon [*sic*]. Harvest Thanksgiving to-morrow evening at Church.

We've had no letter from anybody lately only from Percy from Blackheath about a fortnight ago, he sent us each a brooch that he bought in France at a place on the Lake of Geneva called St. Guigolph (I think that's the word) he says there is a local industry of imitation pearls. You may have heard from him.

Flo says tell Marjorie the machine needles are never for the Bradbury Machines, I don't think they are quite so long. Flo seems to have had a lovely * with you all & feeling ever so much better for the change.

I've lit no fire yet. Flo does the clearing up before breakfast & the upstairs work after breakfast, Mrs. Burton comes Fri & Sat ....

* Word missing here – could be 'time'.
Flo was Mrs. Copping's step-daughter – Joe's step-sister.

TRAVELS WITH JOE COPPING

Joe was not very keen on flying, so chose to travel whenever possible by long-distance coach. He always went with Leroy Travel and enjoyed been seen off from Victoria Coach Station by Louis Leroy, the owner. If you booked more than three holidays with the firm you got preferential treatment with choice of coach seat. Eventually Joe had been with them so many times that he got a free holiday!

In 1960 he asked me to join him on the Leroy holiday to see the Passion Play at Oberammergau. I was suffering from a nervous breakdown when the time came to travel and wanted to back out. Fortunately he persuaded me to go. By the time we reached Ulm I was feeling rotten. Joe ordered me an alcoholic drink of his own concoction and packed me off to bed. Next morning I felt fine and had no more trouble!

Our coach party was very pleasant and select, being composed mainly of clergymen and their ladies. 'I can't get away from them', Joe complained. We travelled first to St. Anton in the Tyrol, where we stayed at the Hotel Valluga: a quiet, traditional Alpine building with comfortable rooms, excellent food and wonderful views. We stayed one night in Oberammergau at the home of Max Flossmann, a house decorator who played cello in the Passion Play orchestra. His wife and twelve-year-old son both had walk-on parts in the play. The boy, like all the males in the performance, had shoulder-length hair, which we found very confusing. A few years later and it would be the fashion in Britain. Joe achieved an ambition in seeing the Passion Play with its long, moving re-telling of the story of the Crucifixion, set against Old Testament flashbacks. It lasted from 10 in the morning until 5 in the afternoon with a two hour lunch break. The morning session was enough for me, and I left Joe to enjoy the afternoon performance with the rest of our party, whilst I explored the hills around the town.

Two years later, in 1962, Joe suggested that we might go to Spain. He adored the sun, but I preferred cooler climes. He eventually persuaded me by choosing a Leroy tour that included a half day's stop at the medieval town of Carcassonne. Our destination was Llorett de Mar, and our fellow travellers were a world removed from those that went to Oberammergau! The coach drove non-stop through the night and we reached Carcassonne at 8.0 a.m. We stopped for toilets and breakfast and then the Courier called us all together. 'We are supposed to stop here 'till midday so that you can see the old ruins' he said, 'but I'm sure you would rather get on to Spain. Is there anyone who objects to going straight on?' There were forty shouts of 'No!'. Joe and I said, 'Yes! We've come specially to see the old town'. A lady with a teenage son plucked up courage and supported us. There were groans from the rest of the party, but we remained adamant, and got our way. The Courier found us a taxi and the four of us had a marvellous morning with an excellent English-speaking guide all to ourselves. When we

Wine Tasting at Llorett de Mar 1962.
Right to left: James Dyer – Joe Copping – 'Adopted' Mother and Son.

returned three hours later the rest of the party were still sitting on the coach. We were ostracised for the remainder of the holiday.

Our hotel at Llorett was very average, with an erratic water supply and no dining room. We ate at a restaurant down the street. When we arrived we were greeted with a delicious freshly-made paella. Our companions rejected most of it and demanded proper food – fish and chips! For the rest of that holiday Joe and I, with the lady and her son (who had by now adopted us), dined 'Spanish' whilst the rest of the mob were served 'British'.

There was nothing to do each day except languish on the beach. By mid-morning even this was too much and we retired to the cool of the hotel until late afternoon. Joe would swim or bake on the beach until he could stand the heat no longer. Before swimming he always removed his half-denture and placed it with his clothes. One morning we had returned to the hotel when Joe realised that he had left his denture on the beach. We hurried back to the by then deserted beach and tried to remember where we had been sitting. The tide was coming in fast and there was some urgency in our task. With amazing good luck we eventually spotted the teeth, coyly nestling amongst the sea-shells, only inches from the advancing water.

In 1964 I decided to go to Brittany with a friend of mine, Ron MacDonald, a fellow teacher and member of the Royal Choral Society. We invited Joe to join us. We stayed at Carnac Ville, with its splendid beach at Carnac Page nearby, where Joe could soak up the sun by the hour. Carnac as a holiday resort was still relatively unknown in 1964. Whilst I went off on archaeological forays Ron chauffeured Joe to the beach and then commuted between us! On two occasions I persuaded Joe to join my antiquarian investigations. We walked at midnight by moonlight along the prehistoric stone avenues and tried to conjure up the spirits of the past. That appealed to his sense of the dramatic. On another I introduced him to a megalithic burial chamber at Crucuno. He went in first, uttered a shriek, and came dashing out. The owner of the adjoining farm had a bull tethered inside. After that Joe refused to visit any more sites with me! It proved an idyllic fortnight, staying in a small hotel which seemed to be staffed entirely by children. They served excellent fresh seafood, cleaned our rooms, manned the reception, and we never saw an adult the whole time we were there. Carnac, when I returned in 1993 had been ruined beyond recognition.

Our final foreign excursion was in 1965 when Joe accompanied Ron and I to Hallstatt in Austria. It was a long car journey and Joe spent it spread-eagled across the back seat, more often asleep than awake. From time to time Ron would break into song. His splendid baritone voice offered a well-known aria, I would add my dubious bass and Joe, depending on his mood, would try anything from soprano to double-bass!

We found Hallstatt breathtakingly beautiful, but we made the mistake of returning via St. Anton only to find a dual-carriageway running through the garden of our once secluded Valluga Hotel. Joe spoke no German but was always game to make the effort. Under no circumstances would he eat cheese, so when it came to ordering the evening meal he always scanned the menu with great caution. He had studied a dictionary before leaving York and had established that the German word for cheese was 'der Kase'. When the waiter came to take his order Joe pointed out his chosen dish and enquired 'Nein kaiser?' The waiter pondered for a moment and then replied in perfect English. 'No Sir, no King nor Emperor either!'

I remember Joe was a great teacher, from whom I learnt most of my craft. When in 1966 I began lecturing in a College of Education he was my model for sound, common-sense teaching. Many were the times when I asked myself, 'What would Joe do in this situation?' His methods are still being used today; passed on by hundreds of former students. Even in the maze that is the National Curriculum there is room for the Copping approach, and generations of children owe their interest in learning to those who were nurtured in Joe's classes at St. John's.

– Remembered by James Dyer 1956-58
3rd March 1996